BACK FROM THE BRINK

BACK FROM THE BRINK

Noel Davidson

AMBASSADOR

Belfast Northern Ireland Greenville South Carolina

Back from the Brink
© Copyright 2000 Noel Davidson

ISBN 1 84030 091 4

Ambassador Publications
a division of
Ambassador Productions Ltd.
Providence House
Ardenlee Street,
Belfast,
BT6 8QJ
Northern Ireland
www.ambassador-productions.com

Emerald House
427 Wade Hampton Blvd.
Greenville
SC 29609, USA
www.emeraldhouse.com

CONTENTS

INTRODUCTION

That afternoon had been an education to me.

For on that afternoon I had gone with Chris Killen to see some of the work in which he was involved, and in the course of our travels we had 'dropped in' on one of the drug addicts with whom he keeps regular contact.

On the way home in the car, Chris explained something of the plight of Northern Ireland's much-bigger-than-I-had-ever-realized group of drug addicts.

"The addicts remind me very much of the man in John five," he said, referring to the Bible story of the powerless man at the Pool of Bethesda. "They have no health, feel they have no hope, and think there is no help. You saw it today. Most of them are miserable. What I want to do," he went on, "is to be the help to them that they so much need. I want to show them that there is hope. That their only hope is in trusting Jesus."

There was nobody better qualified to tell them either.

Chris Killen had been in the same situation himself, as many of them were in now. He knew exactly what they were going through.

Having left home as a schoolboy, Chris had soon become involved in the shady sub-culture of skinhead gangs, booze binges, and drug addiction.

He married Linda, and they had a baby daughter, Samantha. And although he loved his wife and baby, it didn't help. In fact, it only made things worse. Convinced that a no-good-alcoholic-drug-addict was neither fit to be a husband, father, son, or anything else, Chris decided to end it all...

He tried to take his own life...

But God intervened, and snatched him back from the jaws of death.

He did that many times, too. When medical staff were trying to repair his badly abused body, Chris Killen had often stared death in the face. But he was always pulled back from the brink...

And what we were talking about that August afternoon was the reason. The God who had spared him from death had a plan for his life.

On one occasion when he was convinced that he could never make it through yet another life-or-death crisis, God used a Christian consultant to lead Chris to Himself...

'God moves in a mysterious way,

His wonders to perform'... wrote William Cowper.

Look out for God's wonders, and His mysterious ways, in this book.

One of them must be the little red Gideon New Testament which had been given to him in school and keeps popping up in the story.

There is Linda, Chris's teenage sweetheart, and now his wife, who just happened to have an aunt who made it her business to pray for him, day and night, wherever he was, or whatever he did.

In addition there are the Christians on the hospital staff, who realized that God was somehow at work in the life of this patient who seemed to be more in the hospital than out of it, so they began to pray for him too.

It goes on and on...

A few years ago Chris felt that God wanted him to work among the hundreds of drug addicts in our province, reaching them where they were, and telling them about the love of God, and new life in Christ. There was an 'open door' he believed. But if he went through that door, what would he find?...

Visiting the now happy Killen home, as I researched this book, I often tried to imagine, while chatting to Chris and Linda, what it had once been like, but couldn't. The transformation has been so total. Drink and drugs are all part of a totally-forgiven, but-never-quite-forgotten, past. They now talk of the vision Chris and some others have for a Christian rehabilitation centre where drug addicts can be offered medical advice and presented with the Gospel...

As you read this book, whoever you are, and wherever you are, it is my earnest prayer, that you will come to realize, if you haven't already done so, that the God who changed Chris Killen's life, can change yours, too.

He can pluck you back from the brink of death, and plant you firmly on the shore of life. For ever.

Noel I. Davidson,
August, 2000.

1

THE EXTRA SPECIAL BOOK

It was hard to fathom.

Young Chris Killen couldn't figure it out. He just couldn't understand the change that had taken place in his mother's life. Or for that matter why she had even thought she needed it in the first place!

May Killen had always been a respectable, upright kind of a person. She attended Church regularly and tried to bring up her family well. Chris had been told and taught all the decent things to do. Share with your friends. Don't fight with the neighbours. Never cheek up to the teacher. Be nice to the dog. It was that kind of a home.

Then she went one night to a summer tent mission in Wallace Park, near where they lived in Lisburn, and came back all changed. She was the same woman, but different somehow. There was a settled but shining radiance about her.

She told her husband and son Chris that she had been 'saved'. Some people call it being 'converted', she explained. But what it really meant was that she had trusted in Jesus Christ as her Saviour.

This change in his mother, this 'being saved', immediately affected her eight-year-old son in two ways. The first of these was in what he had begun to notice her doing in the home. And the second was in where she began to take him to, out of it!

It came as a kind of a surprise to Chris to see his mother reading the Bible a lot now, for she had never done that before. Indeed it had often been a scramble to find a Bible for everybody in their household before the family outing to Church at Christmas or the Harvest Thanksgiving Service. Now mother was sitting reading it at every spare moment. And it seemed as though she really wanted to, as well. It didn't seem to be any sort of a problem for her. But it was for Chris. A real puzzle. Who would want to read the Bible for prolonged periods? Every day?

Chris had never been all that keen on school. Learning tables and reading books. He had no time for things like that.

Playing football and riding his bike he found much more pleasant. He had more time for things like that.

So to read as much as his mum had started to do, and at the Bible too, that he found odd. Strange. Peculiar.

With the Bible reading there came the praying, as well. This was another new development. His mother, whom he had never seen praying before, now began to tell him that she was praying for him every day. That God would save him soon also.

Chris didn't mind that. He was sure it was good to have her praying for him, and it kept her happy there couldn't be much harm in it. And she surely seemed to be happy!

The other change that took place in the pattern of life for young Chris Killen was that his mother began to expect him to go out to church with her. Every single Sunday. And she expected him to go to Sunday School every week as well.

Chris didn't really mind the Sunday School too much. A kind lady called for him and took him to Great Victoria Street Baptist Church Sunday School in Belfast. The chat with the other children in the car on the seven mile journey was fun, and the Bible stories in the class were interesting.

It was there that the young boy learnt a number of Christian choruses.

It was there that he learnt a number of Bible verses.

It was there that he was clearly and systematically presented with the message of the Gospel.

And it was there, too, that he discovered why his mum had started to read the Bible so much. His Sunday School teachers seemed to place a lot of emphasis on it. They appeared to base all their lessons, whether about God and His love, about Jesus and His death on a cross, or about heaven and hell, on it. It seemed to be their only textbook. It looked as if the Bible was the sole and singular reference book of their belief.

Then when he was just over nine years old Chris saw something strange. It was something which made a lasting impression on him. An image that stayed with him. And the amazing thing was that the other boys who were with him at the time didn't even know that he had seen it!

It happened when two of his friends invited him out to their home, in the village of Lambeg, outside Lisburn, to play one Saturday.

As they were 'messing about', as they called their important-to-them but apparently-pointless-to-anybody-else activity, they discovered what remained of a car which had been involved in an accident. It had been pushed off the side of a road at a junction. Probably awaiting the arrival of the scrap-metal-man's truck to tow it away and squash it flat. It was a total wreck. A write-off. A shell. It had obviously caught fire after a crash for it was both bashed up and burnt out.

It was while the three friends were studiously examining that blackened mass of mangled metal, peering under the buckled bonnet and in through the glassless windows, discussing with childish sincerity what they thought had happened to the car and its occupants, that Chris noticed something.

Although there was hardly anything left of the car, there was something left on what had once been its rear window shelf.

It was a book.

The book was open.

And the book was a Bible.

It was scorched around the edges. The outsides of the pages were charred and crinkly-crisp. The black cover was even blacker, and blistered.

But the Bible hadn't been burnt! In a fire which had reduced a car to a pile of scorched scrap!

There must be something extra special, maybe even magic, about a book like that, the little lad concluded.

2

MAGIC MUSHROOMS

There was great excitement in the Killen household.

Chris had passed 'The Eleven Plus' and been offered a place at Wallace High School, Lisburn. Great.

Father and mother were so pleased. Now Chris would, they were sure, follow in the footsteps of his two elder brothers, Clifford and Trevor, who were, in quietly-proud parental parlance, 'doing quite well for themselves'. Big brother Clifford had made it really big-time. He had always been talented in music, and was by then playing, and touring, with the B.B.C. Symphony Orchestra.

Wouldn't it be wonderful if something like that would turn up for Chris, too?

It would have been wonderful. But it didn't work that way.

Young Chris Killen of eleven-coming-on-twelve had different ideas.

He didn't have the same enthusiasm for school work, or the same ambition to succeed, as either Clifford or Trevor.

To him school was a place where you went to 'muck about' with your friends. And study was a tremendously boring waste of time.

How many people were ever going to ask him, on the streets of Lisburn, for the square root of ten thousand or the date of the Boston Tea Party? And what did he care, either, about Archimedes' Principle or Milton's poetry?

To him all this stuff was nonsense. Rubbish. Vanity and vexation of spirit.

During that first year at 'Wallace', Chris was challenged, though. Compelled to consider himself, and his relationship with God. In two different ways.

The first of these came when he was presented with a Gideon New Testament in the morning assembly. For some reason, which he couldn't immediately explain, that little burgundy book became important to him at once. And he began to read bits of it. At home, in spare moments, and in secret.

Then after a month or two, he stopped.

Real men don't read red Testaments. He thought.

A different, and altogether more frightening experience came later in the year. For it was then that Chris found himself confronted with the realities of life. And death. And whatever lies beyond.

It happened when two girls fell into a fast-flowing river when he was in the same group as them, on a school trip to the Lake District. There was tremendous, but brief, panic until they were safely rescued, and tremendous, but lasting, relief when they were.

When one of the teachers in charge of the party saw that Chris had been visibly 'shaken up' by the incident he began to witness to the concerned pupil. He told him how he could be certain of peace and contentment in this life, and how to be sure of a place in heaven in the life beyond. No matter what happened. Or when it happened. The only source of satisfaction, he said, was to trust in Jesus Christ as your Saviour. To become a Christian.

Chris had heard this often before. In Sunday School. At Church. From his mother. But he had chosen to ignore it. And would do so again.

He was going to have a good time. He thought.

He was going to enjoy all that life had to offer. Just whatever that was. He thought.

From he had started Grammar School, Chris had always gravitated towards boys who were older than himself, for company. Lads who were in the higher forms. And not the work-hard-in-school, play-rugby-'til-you-drop, then-go-home-and-do-your-homeworks lads, either.

It was with the boys who spent most of their evenings just loafing around in the parks and open spaces of Lisburn that Chris began to associate. And it was there, too, and with them, that Chris began to smoke. And then to drink.

Although he knew that his parents wouldn't approve, Chris wanted to appear macho. One of the lads. He was no wimp. If they could do it, so could he. So he smoked his first cigarette. And drank his first can of beer.

Soon smoking and drinking were regular practices for the aimless, idling early-teenager.

It wasn't long until his anxious parents suspected that the company Chris was keeping was not exactly the group of lads they would have hand-picked as his companions, and that he was engaged in such definitely money-squandering and potentially health-hazarding activities as smoking and drinking. So they challenged him about it.

They were becoming increasingly worried about their son. They wanted to do their best for him, and see him do his best for himself.

Chris, however, didn't appreciate either their concern or their challenge.

If anything, their expressed anxiety only made him worse. More defiant. More rebellious. Much more determined to go his own way. And 'do his own thing'.

It was with his pals-in-the-park, too, that Chris had his first experience of drugs. And the effects of drugs and drug-taking on the body and the mind. It was from them that he first heard of the fantastic 'highs' to be had with the so-called 'magic mushrooms'.

A number of the older lads knew where these mushrooms could be picked in the countryside. So they showed their eager-to-experiment younger friend what they were like. And where they were to be had.

This was all so new and so exciting. So exhilarating. Away from the nagging of home, and away from the nuisance of school, out in the countryside. Picking mushrooms.

When he had picked as many as he thought he needed or as many as he could possibly find, his mushroom mentors instructed him in what to do next. After picking, the second step in the process was drying. The long, thin, black-brown fungi had to be placed in a hot spot until they became crumbly crisp.

Chris conducted his drying operations with a high degree of covert caution. He didn't fancy attempting to explain away the presence of the rows of mouldering mushrooms on the shoe-box lid behind the pile of towels in the hotpress, to his mother!

On his first few encounters with 'the magic mushrooms' Chris took thirty or forty at a time. That was, his mates assured him, about 'the recommended dose'.

This gave Chris what was described as 'a good trip'. Every time he took about forty of these dried mushrooms he was possessed by a terrific, but transient, sense of well-being.

The mushrooms affected the senses of the user in an incredible way. Sight and sound particularly, became contorted. Colours became more vivid. Ordinary familiar hues of ordinary everyday objects glowed with an extraordinary unfamiliar luminosity.

It was strange. Creepy. Scary.

The mind also was affected. On some of his first 'good trips' Chris experienced fanciful, almost freakish, dreams. He found himself, in these outlandish visions, doing weird and crazy things. Once he was shooting a pink elephant with a bazooka, in some steamy tropical jungle. Another time he was hacking horrendous huge and hairy spiders to pieces with a hatchet. On the surface of the moon.

All these incredible adventures were invariably accompanied by prolonged fits of hysterical, uncontrollable laughter. Unrestrained and unexplained.

Those were the 'good trips'. And they only lasted a few hours. Three at the most.

There was one day though, when Chris and his pals decided to a hold a 'magic mushroom party'. There had been a good crop of mushrooms which had been picked and 'processed'. Ready for a really big 'bash'.

It was impossible to count the number of hallucinogenic mushrooms that Chris Killen took that afternoon. He must have taken at least two hundred. And so also did some of his friends.

The mushrooms were there. And so was the challenge.

The boys kept goading each other on.

"Go on. I dare you, take some more," someone prompted

"You're not chicken, are you?" another taunted.

"Go on. I dare you, take some more," someone repeated.

"Come on. Let's finish them," another half-high teenager cackled crazily.

When the afternoon's rations were finished Chris Killen set out to walk home. But he was now in an unreal, mind-blown world. His idiotic laughter echoed all along the road. He guffawed loudly at anything any of his friends said. And he collapsed into absolute convulsions at anything he said himself.

As he staggered up the footpath towards home the whole world around him had become contorted. It was like walking through The Hall of Mirrors with every mirror having a different distorting effect, but all at once.

The lamp standards appeared to bend graciously into the middle of the road. Bowing they were, paying homage, to Happy King Chris.

The people one meets on the pavements of Anytown, on Anyday, come in all sorts of general shapes and sizes. But the people Chris met on his magic-mushroom homeward journey came in all sorts of gruesome and grotesque shapes and sizes.

Fat squat men with no heads were followed by tall skinny women with two.

One young mother pushing a pram suddenly became a whole procession of young mothers pushing prams. The fantastic and phenomenal thing about these prams, though was that they seemed to increase in size, and change in colour, the farther away they were. The original young mother with her original pram appeared like a miniature model. A cardboard cut-out in a toyshop. The young mothers in the distance, wheeling luminescent prams as large as lorries, resembled housewives on their way home from a shopping trip in Brobdingnag, Gulliver's mythical land of giants.

On arriving home, Chris had no desire to encounter either of his parents in that state, so he crept quietly past the nearly-closed living-room door, and up to his bedroom.

And it was there, and then, that he became really scared stiff.

For in that room, for twenty minutes, he was transposed, in his mind, from the world of normality and reality into a satanic realm of fiendish fantasy.

As Chris stood swaying in the familiar surroundings of his own bedroom, his attention was attracted to the flowery spread covering his bed. He gazed in stunned disbelief as the flowers on the patterned spread appeared to grow up out of the bed. There were sturdy stalks thrusting up below each flower. As these blooms, in a range of glowing colours, pushed up steadily towards the ceiling, they seemed to wave in the wind. Bow and bend in the breeze.

Raising his eyes above the bedspread flowerbed Chris glanced across at the opposite wall.

And if the blossoms on the bed had been sinister what he saw across the room was shocking.

The walls had begun to bleed!

Thick clots of dark red blood had begun to ooze from black cracks at various levels on the wall. It splurged slowly downwards staining the wallpaper with its own peculiar pattern of thin, sticky, straight lines, in the process. On reaching the floor all these tributary trickles combined to congeal into one revolting river of crimson blood.

It was frightening.

In desperation, Chris flung himself down on the bed, which he knew to be still there. And he closed his eyes as tightly as he could. His valiant attempt to shut out the visionary world around him proved in vain, however. For it only served to launch him into an even more scary, spooky world of imagination. And intimidation.

Ghoulish, ghastly, hellish creatures zoomed down into his face. Their blood-curdling screams besieged his brain.

It was horrifying. Horrendous.

Chris Killen was only fourteen years old, and he was totally terrified.

What had he done?

What was going to happen to him?

What could he do?

Unable to stay in his bedroom any longer Chris obeyed a natural instinct. He did something which he had done often when he had been frightened as a four year old, but never dreamed he would do as a 'macho man' of fourteen. He left his bedroom and hurried downstairs. To his mother. If he had caring company perhaps the evil imaginations in his mind would somehow vanish.

Trying to appear as casual as possible, Chris sat down opposite his mother, and she, as mothers seem to want to do all the time, started to ask probing questions.

They seemed to chase each other out of her mouth, in rapid succession...

"Where have you been, son?"

"Who were you with?"

"What have you been doing?"

"You look a bit pale. Do you feel O.K.?"

Chris sat still for a few moments. Then he took a few deep breaths and attempted to answer some of her queries. But it was difficult.

His voice and his vision had both been affected by his earlier indulgences.

One moment he found himself speaking slowly, in a deep bass voice. Then suddenly, without warning, he would change to speaking quickly, in a high-pitched squeaky voice.

One moment his mother seemed so close to him. Her face seemed to be almost touching his. Then suddenly she seemed so far away. Their twelve foot living-room seemed half-a-mile across.

It didn't take May Killen long to realize that there was something seriously amiss with Chris. He couldn't talk sense. He looked so wretched. The most disturbing thing of all, for her, though, was his eyes. They had a strange, wild, faraway look about them.

"What's wrong with you, Chris?" she asked, suddenly alerted by alarm.

"What's wrong, son?" she repeated anxiously, jumping up from her seat.

"It must be the mushrooms," her by-now-feeling-sick and still-feeling-scared son was forced to confess. "I have taken some magic mushrooms."

The anxious mother sprang into action. Calling her husband she instructed him to take Chris to Lisburn's Lagan Valley Hospital without delay.

When the hospital staff saw the state of the fourteen year old lad who had been rushed in to them, and heard his story, they set to work at once, pumping out his stomach. Time, they knew, was vital. There was always the possibility that this patient had mistakenly taken some potentially poisonous fungi in the course of the 'magic mushroom party'.

Chris spent that night in hospital. In misery.

He lay still for a short period, then shot up into a sitting position, and screamed. And screamed. And screamed.

There were a number of times during the night when he felt so ill that he was convinced he was going to die.

"This is it," he told himself more than once. "I'm finished now. I am going to die. And I'm not ready to meet God."

He pulled through the night, however, and was released later on the next day, when the fearsome effects of the magic mushrooms had worn off.

As he walked out of the hospital with his father who had been so loyal to him, never once leaving his bedside all through the night, young Chris Killen felt miserable.

He was such a flop. Such a failure. Such a fool.

"I will never touch those things again", he promised himself.

But would he, COULD he, keep that promise?

3

CHEERIO! I'M AWAY!

It worked. For a while, anyway.

Chris stayed off the magic mushrooms. But he couldn't escape the call of the culture.

He continued to drink. He continued to smoke. And those were the start of the days of the skinhead. It was the thing to do at that time, to show that you cared not for authority, be it either from home, school, or anywhere else, to have all your hair shaved off. Become a skinhead.

So Chris had it done. One of his friends performed the honours, acted as barber. And Chris Killen arrived home that night with his head shaved and shining. The startling white of his scalp stood out in stark contrast to his dark clothing. It just looked like a big peeled onion impaled on a pitch-black post.

His parents were disappointed. And disgusted.

The skinhead caused a terrible row at home.

The school authorities were outraged. And disgusted.

So the skinhead caused a terrible row, but also instant retribution, at school.

This insolent rebel couldn't be permitted to contaminate the other seven hundred or so conscientious pupils at the school. So Chris was given his lessons, and his lunch, alone.

When his hair started to grow back and the skin on Chris's head began to resemble that of a baby hedgehog rather than that of a great white whale, the position at home became more peaceful. And the situation at school became more normal. As normal as it could be, perhaps, in an institution dedicated to the teaching of everything, with a responsibility towards a pupil who was neither interested in, nor dedicated to, the learning of anything.

Then, during the Christmas holiday, the crunch came. The big decider. Not make or break time. Just big break time.

One night, in a friend's house, Chris shaved a friend's head. Left him a skinhead.

And by way of a big thank you gesture for his efforts with the razor, the friend returned the compliment. By giving Chris a Mohican. He shaved all his mutinous mate's hair off at either side, leaving only a two-inch-wide cockscomb on top, running from front to back. Then, just in case anyone should miss his Mohican, Chris dyed what remained of his hair, the crest across the crown, bright orange!

When he arrived home later on that evening there was a row. Not a small, insignificant, if-you-do-that-again-I-will-have-to-tell-your-daddy kind of row. This was a big row. A blazing row. A row to end all rows. Upstairs on the landing.

"This is a respectable area, Chris!" his father fumed. "You can't come in and out around here looking like that! Whatever will the neighbours think of you?! Or of us?!"

May Killen just cried. She wept a lot more, but said a lot less, than her husband. The few comments she did make, though, showed that she felt more let down than indignant. She was more sad than mad.

"Oh, Chris, why are you doing these things to us?" she wailed woefully at one stage. "Why? Why? Why?"

As his father persisted in pursuing his 'What a big disgrace you are' and 'You can't live here looking like that!' topic, something snapped in the mind of young Chris Killen.

"O.K. then! All right!" he bellowed like a bull. "If I can't live here looking like this, then I WON'T live here looking like this. Cheerio! I'm away!"

With that he leapt down the stairs four at a time and hurtled out into the night, banging the front door after him with such venom that the whole house shuddered and shook. Then, when he was gone, it settled into a stunning, sickening silence.

Although he didn't realize it at the time, Chris Killen had just turned his back on the two people who cared most for him in the whole world. But he didn't care much for them at that particular moment. He had made a snap decision to rid himself of all the moaning and moping. Free himself from all the finicky fussiness. Why should he have to listen to them whingeing all the time?

He would go somewhere. Do something. Live free. Hang loose.

At fifteen-coming-sixteen he was well able to look after himself, he reckoned.

At two o'clock in the morning Chris Killen was walking alone on the streets of the Knockmore Estate in Lisburn. It was mid-winter. And bitterly cold.

Eventually he realized that he couldn't stay out, wandering about, all night. He would have to find shelter somehow. Somewhere. There was one of his friends who could help him, he thought. For he slept in a downstairs bedroom, he knew.

When Chris went round to his friend's house and knocked on the window a somewhat startled, but still rather sleepy, face peered out between the curtains. On seeing who it was, at his window in the middle of the night, and on hearing the story that Chris had to tell, the awakened sleeper opened the window and Chris half-climbed and was half-pulled, into the bedroom. And it was there that Chris remained until morning, lying, but not sleeping, on the floor.

Next morning, after some earnest contemplation, Chris and his friend decided that the best place for the turbulent teenager to stay was with another friend who had more room and less restrictions, over at his place.

So it was there that Chris went to stay.

And it was to there, too, that his distraught mother traced him, later on in the day.

The first piece of news that she had to bring to Chris seemed to be upsetting her badly. But it didn't worry her son at all. To him it was a real relief.

"When I phoned the School this morning to tell them that you had a Mohican haircut, and that you had run out on us, do you know what they said, Chris? Do you know what they said?" mother asked, in a vain attempt to prick the conscience of her renegade son.

"No, what did they say?" Chris enquired, casually. He wasn't really in the slightest bit concerned what they had said, but it seemed to be important to his mother. And he sometimes felt sorry for her.

"They said that if you have a Mohican haircut you are not to go back! They are expelling you!" mother replied. She had worked herself into a frenzy, and the last few words of her exclamation were drowned in a sort of sobbing shriek.

"I'm not surprised at that!" Chris retorted, defiantly. "And I don't care either! To tell you the truth I had decided not to go back there anyway. Only a waste of time that!"

Then mother came to the purpose of her visit. The reason for the mission.

"Even though you are not going back to school will you come back home with me, son?" she begged him, her eyes red and swollen with intermittent bouts of weeping. "You CAN live in our house, in our neighbourhood, in spite of what was said last night. We didn't mean to put you out you know!"

"You said I couldn't live in that neighbourhood looking like this, and I'm sure you meant it," Chris replied. He was still angry. And still adamant. "And I look exactly the same now as I did last night. So I am not going back. They have told me I can stay here as long as I like, so this is where I will be staying!"

"Please! Please! PLEASE!" mother pleaded.

"No! No! NO!" Chris retorted.

His mother left, later, just exactly as she had arrived, earlier.

Alone, and heart-broken.

4

A BATHFUL OF BEER

After a few weeks Chris relented.

He did go home. For although he hated to admit it to himself, the relative luxury of his own heated bedroom, the regular supply of nourishing food and the reassuring stability of tender loving care, proved too attractive to resist.

His stopover at home was short, however. For although he tried to tell himself that he was better off there than anywhere else he could ever be, the call of the world outside kept ringing in his ears.

'You ought to be out here', it said repeatedly.

'Get out here and start enjoying yourself', it urged endlessly.

' What's a macho man like you doing stuck at home with his mammy and daddy?' it mocked mercilessly.

And before Easter 1982 Chris heeded that call. Gave in to those taunts. He left home again to join some lads from Lisburn who were planning to travel to Portrush for the holiday weekend.

On Good Friday evening Chris and his cronies descended upon the North Antrim resort. They were all high on drugs and in a drunken stupor when they arrived off the train. And they drank, and remained drunk, for the next two days.

Then on Easter Monday, in the company of dozens of other skinheads and discontents, they proceeded to wreck the town. By the end of the day Portrush was littered with broken bottles, broken windows, and broken windscreens. There were broken hearts too, lots of them, as sickened shopkeepers surveyed the damage to their property.

And for a while after that weekend of wanton destruction Chris went home. Again.

Despite the best efforts at kindness and care by his mother and the best efforts at forgiveness by his father, however, Chris didn't feel at home, at home.

There now seemed to be planted within him a ceaseless restlessness. A renegade rebellious spirit. Chris Killen wanted to live rough with those living rough. And act tough with those acting tough. Be as foul-mouthed or as full-drunk as he liked. Where and when he pleased.

So in June 1982 he ran away from home once more. This time it was going to be for good, he had determined. He wasn't going to succumb to the pull of the comforts of home or the pathos of the cries of his mother again. No way. He was a tough guy now. After all was he not almost sixteen years of age?!

He could handle himself. Anywhere. Or any time. Or with anybody. Or so he thought.

Chris and two of his skinhead pals rented a run-down flat in the Mount Vernon area of north Belfast. And there they stayed, camping rather than living. It was a crude, basic existence.

White bread and drugs were their staple diet.

A bathful of beer was their only drink. When supplies ran low one or two of the residents robbed a wine shop somewhere, and they replenished the beer in the bath. If a stock up was needed for a midday breakfast or a midnight party one of the three teenage tenants dipped a rusty old mop bucket into the bath and brought it back into the living room, leaving it to drip all over the filthy floor. Then anybody who happened to be able to find a glass or mug, either clean or dirty, dipped it in the bucket and drew off what he needed.

They all took drugs. All sorts of drugs.

The three lads who stayed in that flat could survive without their dinner but they could not survive without their drugs. Their body craved another, and another and yet another fix. If they couldn't afford to buy them, which they couldn't, they were driven to stealing to obtain them. Which is what they did

As winter approached, and the days became shorter and the nights longer, Chris and his friends became largely nocturnal in habit. They spent the day asleep all over the flat and spent the night at parties all over the city. And getting there was part of the party too. They thought nothing of walking six or seven miles to a bash over in south Belfast, generally making a nuisance of themselves, all along their route.

While the functions of day and night were reversed in their lifestyle the day of the week had no significance whatsoever. Saturday or Sunday, Monday or Tuesday, it made no difference. They neither went to work or went to church. They only went to pubs or parties. Every night of the week.

It was when he was almost seventeen years of age, having spent a year in Mount Vernon, that this reckless, careless, fearless life-style almost cost Chris his life. He and a crowd of friends had been to hear the skin-head band 'Offensive Weapon' playing in the White Horse bar off Royal avenue, in Belfast's city centre. This band and the message of its music were extremely popular with its fanatical fanclub. Indeed, some of its followers, including Chris, had the words 'Offensive Weapon' tattooed across their totally hairless heads. To them those band members were idols. Heroes. Leaders of a reactionary but necessary cult.

It was on the way home from that gig in the early hours of the following morning, when passing the fiercely republican Unity Flats that Chris and his fiercely loyalist skinhead friends became embroiled in a violent, no-holds-barred, bottles-and-bricks, fists-and-feet confrontation with 'the other side'.

When the Mount Vernon gang thought they were winning, and were convinced that they had put the enemy to flight, they began to chase them back into their territory. It was a mistake. For it was an old military stratagem. And a simple trick.

When Chris and his crowd of brick and insult hurling heroes advanced deeper into the heart of their opponents enclave the enemy-on the -run called up reinforcements from eerie entries and all sorts of alleyways.

Then they turned on their pursuers.

Some of his friends saw what was happening and beat a hasty retreat. Just in time to avoid capture. And a brutal beating.

Chris was not so fortunate.

He was caught and attempted to fight his way out.

It was all to no avail, however.

He had taken too much to drink down in The White Horse, and although this had boosted his loyalist ego it had dulled his senses and sapped his strength.

Chris was knocked unconscious.

The dishevelled figure lay face down in the road. Motionless. His skinhead was spattered and streaked with his own congealing blood. He had been kicked black and blue.

Although his fellow-fighters had escaped relatively unscathed they knew that they couldn't just walk away and leave Chris lying there. They weren't sure of the extent of his injuries, and were afraid that he might die.

So when they were as sure as they could be that the coast was clear they crept furtively up to their still-comatose companion, and dragged him to safety.

Then they phoned for an ambulance.

Chris Killen regained consciousness, head swathed in bandages and aching every where it was possible for a body to ache, it seemed. He was in Mater Hospital. But hadn't a clue how he ever got there!

At visiting time, his mother, his next-of-kin who had been contacted, arrived up to see him.

She was shocked and shaken when she saw the state of her prodigal son.

Her maternal instinct made her long to have him home to nurse him back to health and fitness again.

It would be great to have a chance to show him just how much she still loved him. Demonstrate practically how much she still cared for him. Spoil him for a while.

"Please Chris will you come home with me, son?" she implored. "Please! Please! PLEASE!"

"No, mother. I will be going back to the guys in the flat when they let me out of here. And I won't be going home again", was her apparently insensitive son's insistent reply. "No! No! NO!"

So mother left that hospital later that day just as she had arrived earlier. And just in the same way as she had left the foul flat in Mount Vernon so many times in earlier days, too.

Alone, and broken hearted.

5

SPECIAL BOOTLACES, STRANGE BAGFELLOWS

When Chris was discharged from hospital, he didn't go home. He had told his mother that he wouldn't. And he didn't. But he didn't go back to the flat in Mount Vernon either.

During his stay in the Mater two of his friends had been visiting, and sowing in his mind the seeds of a plan they were hatching. It was to do with expanding their horizons. Extending their sphere of influence. And seeing more of their special scene.

If he was willing enough, when he was well enough, these two trailblazers proposed that Chris should join them on a trip to London.

London!

It sounded great. And big. And magical, somehow.

He could be so much more free, and have so much more fun, if he was in London. No mother popping in every now and again sobbing her heart out, begging him to come home. And an endless supply of drink and drugs. Not to mention the bigger and 'better' variety of skinhead bands to be found over there.

A trip or two to London would give him a chance to become even more extreme in his views. And even more violent in his actions.

So Chris accepted his friends' invitation. And joined them on a trip to London.

His first impressions of the seamier side of the nation's capital, were very much as he had expected them to be. There were a number of skinhead bands playing in selected pubs and clubs of the sprawling metropolis, and Chris went, or was taken, to hear many of them.

They sounded inspired to him. The underlying message of their music, its unashamed and unrestrained vitriolic hatred, pleased him well. And the more bitter the better.

After a few weeks initial scouting around Chris became friendly with Ian Stewart who was the lead singer with Skrewdriver, a leading skinhead band. And Ian Stewart was a ranting radical reactionary.

It wasn't long until Chris Killen had become part of a gang, and a culture, which believed it was their mission on earth to purge the planet of anybody who didn't belong to its white Protestant population. This was his only religion. His ultimate goal. His reason for living.

To help play his part in the ethnic cleansing of the capital, Chris joined the National Front. To him it wasn't sufficient to be merely an unidentified member of that out-and-out organization, however. He had to demonstrate his allegiance. By his distinctive dress. And brutish behaviour.

Chris wore an earring in his left ear.

For the unwritten code stated that left was for loyalist. And right was for republican.

And he was most decidedly loyalist. Most certainly not republican.

It was very important to him that everybody was well aware of that.

Chris had two lines shaved in the stubble that covered the left side of his head.

For the unwritten code stated that those with two lines on the left were loyalist. Those with one line on the left were republican.

And he was most decidedly loyalist. Most certainly not republican.

About this, he felt it was important, that no-one was in the slightest doubt.

Chris always wore thick white bootlaces in his heavy laced-up-the-shin black boots.

For the unwritten code stated that long white bootlaces in long black boots identified the wearer as a follower of The National Front. And Chris was a fully-fledged member. A devoted disciple.

And wanted it to be widely known.

Such were the signs of the times, that if Chris and his gang of white-laced-boot boys ever encountered, on the streets of London, a gang of yellow-laced-boot boys, they began to hurl abuse, and just about anything else that came in anyway handy, at them. For yellow-laced-boot boys were anti-National Front. And sworn enemies.

During those days of life in London Chris made irregular, and somewhat reluctant, trips home. But he had to. It was not a matter of choice, very often. But a means of survival.

London proved to be an expensive choice of location in which to shoot your dope or fight your cause, and Chris often found himself broke. Practically penniless.

When this happened, when he had drunk or drugged himself down to his last pound, he invariably phoned home. Appealing for funds.

And the answer he received from his long-suffering, loving mother was invariably the same, also.

"We will send you a little something to keep you going if you wish, son," she would promise. Then she would pause for a moment, and out of a powerful silence pop in the proviso, "But if you would spend it on your fare home, then we could give you so much more!"

There were times when Chris settled for the 'something to keep him going', but discovered that it wasn't long until he was back in the telephone kiosk again pleading for something more. Just to keep him going a little longer.

On other occasions, however, he responded to his ever-patient mother's apparently sensible suggestion. And came home.

These return trips to Lisburn were usually of a brief but profitable nature. Chris spent a week or ten days stocking up with food and money, and tolerating some genuine tender loving care, then set off again. Back across the Irish Sea. Clutching his very-much-the-worse-for wear holdall.

Inside that battered black bag which Chris carried on all his trips home and back, laid carefully across the bottom so that nobody would see them, were two items of luggage. Two items of luggage which were as different in their projected purpose as it would be possible for any two inanimate objects to be. They seemed to scream out at each other, so sharp was the contrast.

One was a machete. A fierce looking African hunting-knife. It just fitted in across the bottom of the bag, not dead straight across, but diagonally, corner to corner.

Chris reckoned the machete could come in useful sometime in the future. For self-defence. Or if perhaps he was ever called upon to stand up and fight in a 'real do', it might even prove valuable. In attack.

An essential bit of skinhead baggage. No matter how you looked at it.

Then there was its incongruous companion. Nestled in hard by the handle of the razor-sharp weapon was a little red Gideon New Testament. It was the one which Chris had been given as a turning turbulent first-year pupil at Wallace High School. It would be useful for something, sometime, too, he was sure.

But he could never quite be sure when. Or for what.

There were rare times when he sneaked it out of its holdall-hideaway and read some of it secretly. He would have been mortified if his mates had found him, in his skinhead N.F. gear, and with his hard-man image, reading the Bible! But he snatched short snippets of it, in lonely moments, when he could.

Again, he was never quite sure why he did this. The runaway teenager found himself at a loss to explain why that, after all he had heard and seen and done, he had never lost his desire to have and handle that little red Testament.

It really was a peculiar mixture of two contrasting components in imprecise proportions. The first element was a deep respect for his caring mother and her Christian beliefs and the second was the need for some sort of a good luck charm. Chris somehow felt that if he read God's Word, then God in turn would feel obliged to smile benevolently on him. Regardless of how actively anti-Christian he had become. Or how many times he took God's holy name in vain.

Slowly, gradually, he began to realize that he had started to feel insecure. There were pangs in his heart and cracks in his dreams. The life in London was beginning to lose its lustre.

Then, on a stock-up visit home to Lisburn in the summer of 1983, Chris met somebody different. Somebody he really liked.

And somebody who was to have an inexplicable influence on him...

6

LINDA

It was late on a Saturday afternoon and Chris was in a car with two of his friends. Their driving repeatedly into, then out of, and generally all around Lisburn's town centre seemed like an aimless exercise, a pointless waste of petrol.

But it wasn't to them.

For Chris and his two pals were 'talent spotting'.

They were 'watching all the girls go by'.

Suddenly Chris 'spotted' someone he fancied. He had noticed her before on two previous circuits, chatting and laughing animatedly but unsuspectingly, with three friends.

When Chris decided that this was a lead worth pursuing he asked the driver to pull in to the edge of the kerb, which he did, just past the girls.

The front seat passenger knew one of the girls, so he rolled down his window.

"Come here a wee minute, Denise," he called out, his tone having more of the urgency of a command rather than the courtesy of a request.

Denise complied and came smiling across to the car. Perhaps she thought that she herself had caught somebody's eye. Could this be her 'big day'?

"See that girl in the middle over there, what's her name?" came the question from the car.

"Oh that's Linda. Linda Castles," Denise replied, trying to appear perky rather than peeved.

The spokesman in the passenger seat decided to press the matter further. "Well, Chris here would like a date with her," he said.

"Oh would he now?!" Denise threw back her head and laughed. "We will have to see what SHE has to say about that!" she retorted, and then returned to the giggling group who had by then retreated a further yard or two, back against the wall of a Bank.

When the intermediary had conveyed her message, Linda dropped her head coyly to the one side and asked, "Chris? Which one is Chris?"

She then leaned over to one side to pretend to peer into the car.

"I think Chris must be the one in the back," Denise told her. She had it worked out, by a process of elimination, that Chris just had to be 'the one in the back'.

After a short period of sniggering, and shuffling shuttle diplomacy, it was arranged that Chris and Linda would meet for their first 'date', later that evening, in Lisburn.

And when Chris met Linda on her own, one-to-one, he liked her instantly.

She was lovely, he thought. So lively. And with such a vibrant personality.

Linda was a good-looker. And a good talker.

But when this boyfriend-on-trial asked her about her age, Linda lied.

"I'm fifteen," she told him confidently, then turned away so that he wouldn't spot the blush that she felt burning on her cheek.

She wasn't fifteen. She was only fourteen, but looked like fifteen. Or even sixteen.

Linda was really keen to impress this would-be tough guy. For under the skinhead hard-man picture he was trying to paint she sensed that there lay a very lovable lad.

The truth was that she liked him from the first moment they met, too. So she didn't want to lose him because he considered her too young.

That Saturday night was the first of a number of pleasant meetings for Chris and Linda. An irresistible attraction for each other had sprung up between them. So their 'dates' became more frequent, and most enjoyable.

This rapidly-blossoming love for Linda soon began to pose a problem for Chris.

One part of him wanted to remain in Lisburn with Linda. And his bike.

The other part, though, the 'enjoy-yourself-however-you-like-wherever-you-like' part, wanted to return to London, to Dolly. And her friends.

Chris had bought himself a second-hand motor-bike during the summer, and he really liked it. Unfortunately, though, his dad wasn't just so fond of it, not that he had anything against motor bikes generally, or even this bike in particular. His main objection to the red and black Yamaha 350 was neither its make or its colour, but what Chris wore every time he went out on it. What really upset him was the fact that each time Chris roared away from the house on that Yamaha he wore a half-cut Wrangler over his leather jacket. And that half-cut Wrangler sported an unmistakable swastika motif. As someone who had served in the armed forces in the Second World War Tommy Killen found this particularly offensive. To him it was but another demonstration of an anti-establishment, anti-everything attitude.

There were rows about it. But that was nothing new.

Chris didn't care, though.

He liked his bike.

And if he liked his bike he loved his Linda.

But although Linda was growing to like Chris more and more every time they met she neither loved nor liked his bike either. She didn't detest it like his dad, but she was afraid of the thing. She was scared stiff by the deafening roar, the potential speed and the raw power. And when Chris climbed on to the saddle of that machine he seemed to be suddenly transformed into a raw-power-mad maniac. Linda didn't understand that, but it bothered her a bit. So she stayed away from the bike, refusing repeated requests to 'come for a spin', on the pillion.

Chris and Linda walked everywhere that summer. They spent many pleasant sunny afternoons and sunset evenings strolling around the busy streets and flower-strewn parks of their home town, chatting, laughing, relaxing. Gradually coming to know, and to like, each other, even better.

It was fun for them both while it lasted.

In late September, however, when the carefree days of summer had become treasured items in the memory bank, and the approaching-autumn days had become noticeably colder and shorter, Chris decided to return to London. For Linda had returned to school.

In the hotel in the capital where he was given bed and breakfast because he was on the dole, and registered 'homeless', Chris renewed his acquaintance with his skinhead friends, who were also on the dole, and registered 'homeless'. And with Dolly.

To Chris, for a while, Dolly had been something of a novelty. She was a curio. A talking point. 'Good for a laugh.'

For this Dolly was a trained monkey, who sat around in the hotel porch, vetting the potential clientele. She had one simple and self-appointed role in life, and she performed it with great gusto.

Anybody white was welcome on the premises, and totally disregarded by Dolly, but she chased with a lot of unnecessary noise, and frightening phony fierceness, any coloured person who dared to step inside the door.

He hadn't been long in London, however, until Chris discovered that the appeal of the country's capital was nowhere nearly as strong for him now as it once had been.

The skinhead bands were still playing and he went to hear them often. As he had done before.

Drugs were still readily available from the usual sources and he used them often. As he had done before.

But there was still something missing. Or was it somebody?

Chris missed Linda, and although they exchanged long and loving letters, he still wanted to see her.

So he came back to Lisburn, and stayed a few weeks.

Then he became unsettled and headed off back to London.

Not long after his return to London he returned to Lisburn yet again, sorely- lacking Linda.

And soon he set off to London once more...

Chris was finding it hard to settle.

There was, he discovered, something sadly lacking in his life.

He had expected to be enjoying himself to the full in London. But he wasn't.

He had thought that the drugs and the bands and the gangs would have given him the same buzz as before.

But they hadn't.

On more than one occasion Chris found himself, in lonely moments, delving down deep into his bag. For the little red Gideon New Testament. He thought that perhaps the answer to his disturbing sense of emptiness and increasing sense of restlessness lay in there somewhere.

But he hadn't found it. Yet.

Late in November Chris left London and went down to stay with his brother Trevor in Portsmouth for a few days.

Perhaps there would be something different to do down there.

But there wasn't.

He spent his days just lounging around in pubs and clubs.

It had gradually all begun to appear so pointless, somehow.

Then something happened which allowed Chris to afford the fare home. On two successive nights he won one hundred pounds on the fruit machines in a gaming club.

This was 'unheard of' before at the club, and a miracle for the lonely lad from Lisburn. For the teenager who was usually 'broke' had suddenly and unexpectedly become relatively rich.   At seven o'clock on Tuesday evening Chris had been wandering around with a few pence short of twenty pounds in his pocket, and when he woke up, at seven o'clock on Thursday morning, he had more than two hundred pounds in that same pocket!

This newly-won wealth allowed him to do two things he had been wanting to do for some time.

He bought Christmas presents, for Linda and his parents.

And he bought a single ticket home, to Linda and his parents.

Thus it was that a disillusioned and seriously-seeking-something Chris Killen arrived home for Christmas on 23rd December, 1983.

Was it only for Christmas, though?

Or would it be for good this time?

7

A PLACE IN THE COUNTRY

Now that Chris was home and seeing more of Linda, he began to realize that motor-bikes were fine for solo spins on sunny summer evenings but were not entirely suitable for taking your girl-friend out on frosty winter nights!

So, early in January, 1984, he applied for, and passed, the driving test, in his dad's car.

Tommy Killen had mixed feelings about this.

It was great that Chris could now drive, for another driver in the family could always prove useful in a time of crisis. The fact that Chris would now probably expect to use the car to take his girl-friend out caused him some minor concern, though. There was always this niggling fear at the back of this mind that Chris would be tempted to 'show off' to Linda, and 'write off' the car. He soon came to accept that risk as an essential hazard, however, and 'the lesser of two evils'. At least it would keep him off 'that dreadful old motor-bike'.

Chris did ask for the use of the family's light blue Ford Escort to take Linda out, just as his dad had anticipated. Father needn't have worried about his son's driving skills, or his defiant year on the Yamaha, though. When Chris had Linda in the car he felt more responsible, and was, as a result, more careful.

After a few nights spent in and around Lisburn and district, Chris and Linda ventured out on their first 'long journey' in the car. To them it was quite an adventure, this expedition up into the country.

It was a Saturday afternoon in early March, and the bravest of buds were beginning to appear in the hedgerows when Chris drove Linda up to visit Violet Lowry, who was an aunt of Linda's mother. Although Violet was Linda's great-aunt, and almost two generations removed from the young couple, the vivacious teenager held the apparently quite elderly lady in high regard. And she was, for some reason, very keen that she should meet Chris. She had a feeling that they would like each other, somehow.

Violet lived in a cottage near Dromara, deep in the heart of rural County Down. The cottage had once-upon-a-time been thatched, but by the time of Chris and Linda's visit it had been brought bang up to date. In regard to the roof, at least. For it was by then covered with shiny sheets of corrugated iron which shimmered in the turning-Spring sunshine.

Linda had many happy memories of many happy holidays that she and her sisters had spent with 'Aunt Violet', as they called her.

There were so many things she had enjoyed. Playing in the hayshed across the lane, was a special treat for a 'townie' like her. The smell of the hay when you walked through it, rolled in it, or just lay on it, was something she had always fondly remembered, but had never been able to adequately describe.

Sitting in the flickering lamplight, just before bedtime, with glowing cheeks after a day spent in the open air, had been special too. The fact that Aunt Violet didn't have 'the electric', didn't worry the visiting Castles girls at all. The oil lamp with its tall glass globe, and the kettle on the range, were things they didn't have at home.

Everything they ate was cooked on the top of a jet-black range which had been somewhat dubiously dubbed, a 'Modern Mistress'. Little Linda, in those earlier days, used to be fascinated to watch

Aunt Violet pour shovelfuls of coal, or drop roughly cut logs, down into the range through a hole she had made in the top by lifting off a lid with a specially designed metal sort-of-claw-shaped implement. Then the frying-pan or a saucepan would be placed on the replaced lid, and soon a meal would be ready. If only hot water was required the ever-present kettle was filled and slid across to the heat. When not in immediate use the kettle just sat steaming away silently to itself in a back corner of the black range.

Although her memories of days down in Dromara were mostly idyllic, there were two aspects of life in that cottage on which Linda had not been all that particularly keen.

One had been a superabundance of something.

And the other was a total lack of something else.

The superabundance was of insects. Linda was often convinced that every conceivable kind of flying or fluttering, buzzing or humming, jumping or crawling creature known to man lived in or around her Aunt Violet's cottage. And she hated them. Loathed them. All of them. They gave her 'the creeps'.

The lack, by contrast, was of an inside 'facility'. The only toilet about the place was 'across the yard', and the girl who until then had taken the minor luxuries of Lisburn-living more or less for granted, didn't like that. She and her sisters were afraid to go out to the toilet in the middle of the night. There might just be 'a mouse, or a moth, or a monster out there somewhere'! The outside toilet was passably O.K. by day, but no matter how late you 'went' in the evening, it always seemed like ages until daylight, and comfort, returned!

Since he had no memory bank to dip into when Chris first visited that cottage in the country that Saturday afternoon, his mind was not preoccupied with a place in the past. It was, though, thoroughly impressed by a person in the present.

And that person was Aunt Violet.

As soon as he stepped out of the car, Chris was touched by the warmth of the welcome he received.

"So this is Chris. I'm really glad to meet you, Chris!" the lady with the straight greying hair turned up into a loose roll which lay easily on the collar of her white blouse, and the friendly smile, said simply, but with patent sincerity.

"Yes. I'm Chris," the ever so slightly embarrassed seventeen-year-old replied. 'What is this very nice lady going to make of a no-good lout like me?' he wondered to himself. 'Am I going to disgrace Linda and my self, here?'

It proved to be an unfounded fear. An understandable, but unnecessary, concern.

Aunt Violet was a Christian. 'A REAL Christian', was how Chris described her to somebody later.

One of the first things Chris noticed when the three of them proceeded into the living-room of Aunt Violet modest home was her big Bible. This well-worn volume, with a pair of reading-glasses folded neatly across it, occupied a prominent position on the corner of the sideboard. The signal seemed to say, 'This Book is read, respected and recognized as the handbook of this house'.

Chris spotted, but didn't need, that specific signal.

Aunt Violet's gentle attitude said the very same thing, Sent out the very same message. 'The Bible is read, and lived out, here.'

As they sat and talked, clustered around the 'Modern Mistress' in comfortable armchairs, Chris noticed that Aunt Violet, who loved to talk, seemed to have difficulty in talking to them. It seemed that every word, in her high-pitched squeaky voice, was the product of more than normal effort. She appeared to be constantly gasping for breath.

"You will have to excuse my funny old voice," she explained at one stage to the young couple who were charmed to bathe in the warmth of her every word, "but I nearly died of T.B. in my teens, so I find talking, and sometimes even breathing, hard at times."

So that was it sorted out. Not that it mattered to Chris. **What** the woman said was infinitely more important to him than **how** she actually said it.

What she said seemed to be always positive. She appeared so interested in Chris, enquiring kindly about his parents and his home, and asking sometimes-hard-to-answer questions about life in London.

Although he was acutely aware that the world of this woman, whose only kick in life seemed to be driving her little car, at thirty miles per hour, to every wee-meeting in every wee-hall in the countryside, was a million miles removed from his world of drink and drugs, Skrewdrivers and Offensive Weapons, Chris somehow felt strangely at ease with her.

They hadn't been talking together very long until he felt that Aunt Violet had known him all his life. And had cared about him for that long as well.

And what it was that she chose **not** to say impressed Chris too.

In all the time they were there, on that first day, Chris never heard Aunt Violet say a harsh word about anybody. When she mentioned somebody it always seemed that it was in a caring, constructive kind of way.

Nor did she say to Linda, as Chris had at first feared she would, "Where did you fall in with a creep like that?"

The statement to crown all statements, and undoubtedly Aunt Violet's most striking statement of an altogether very satisfying day, came later in the evening, when Chris and Linda were leaving for home.

They were both in the car, preparing to drive away. Chris wound down his window to allow them all to say their last 'Good-byes'.

It was then that Aunt Violet leaned forward, and resting her arms on the inch of glass left protruding, looked Chris in the eye and remarked, "It has been really great to meet you Chris. I will be praying for you. I have been praying for Linda since she was born. Now I will add you to my list."

She then stepped back a few paces from the car, smiled sweetly, and said simply, "'Bye!"

As they set off down the road Chris and Linda sat in a sort of a stunned and sacred silence for a short time.

Both of them were touched.

They had encountered on a Saturday afternoon visit, to the heart of the country, a genuinely caring Christian.

And she had promised 'to pray for' them both, too.

That, they reckoned, could only be good.

8

OVERDOSE

For more than a year Chris and Linda saw each other regularly and towards the end of 1985 decided that they wanted to be married. Since they were determined to spend the rest of their lives together they reckoned that it would be the only right and sensible thing to do.

Since Chris had never worked in any permanent employment, and thus had little or no money, and since both sets of parents considered them to be, 'still so very young', they decided to have a quiet wedding. A simple ceremony.

So Chris and Linda were married on Friday, 6th December 1985, in St. Columba's Presbyterian Church in Lisburn. It was a small family wedding with a small family reception to follow. And even though Chris had been drinking alcohol for the previous six or seven years, so much so that it had become an ingrained ingredient of his lifestyle, both he and Linda agreed unanimously that there would be no alcohol at their reception. Their reason for this was quite simple.

It might offend Aunt Violet. And the last thing either of them would ever want to do was offend Aunt Violet. For they held her in such high esteem. She was such a lovely caring Christian, who assured them at the reception, as they had expected she would, that she would be 'continuing to remember' them in prayer.

After the wedding the newly married couple moved in to live with Chris's parents. This it was hoped would only be a temporary measure for they had applied to the authorities for a house but hadn't as yet been granted one.

'Your names are on the waiting list', was what they were told. Time and time again.

Then later in the next year, 1986, Chris and Linda faced the first real test of their love and devotion. And their capacity to cope.

This came when their first baby, Samantha, was born, seven weeks premature. Their little baby, who weighed just over four pounds, had to be rushed off to the Jubilee Maternity Hospital in Belfast, to be placed in an incubator. Her life was in danger. It was just 'touch and go' as to whether or not she would survive.

Chris and Linda, the young parents, travelled into Belfast to the hospital to see her, twice a day. Every day.

It was with mixed emotions that they viewed baby Samantha in her incubator.

It was thrilling to realize that this was their very own baby, their very own daughter, but it was upsetting to see her, too. She was so tiny and so fragile to have all those tubes around her. The hospital staff kept telling them that she was doing as well as could be expected. But still they were worried. In slightly different ways

Linda, as a mother, worried for her baby. She wanted Samantha to survive. To be well. And to grow up into a normal, healthy girl.

Chris worried too.

He worried about all the same things as Linda, but he had also some more personal concerns. And convictions. And an ever-accusing conscience.

Baby Samantha had been in her incubator in the Jubilee Hospital for more than a week when the young parents came home from visiting her one evening, and the young father was very depressed.

Linda stayed downstairs talking to his parents, answering all their anxious 'How did you find Samantha tonight?' type questions, but Chris wanted to be away from them all. He couldn't bear to talk to anybody. He was so dejected.

For days he had been feeling miserable. But that night he felt especially useless.

Life for him had become aimless. Pointless. Fruitless. Futile.

He went up into his brother Clifford's bedroom, flopped down on the bed, and began to think things over.

As he contemplated his life up until that date, Chris Killen came to the conclusion that he was no good. Everything he had done, or had ever tried to do, had been a mess. A shambles. A waste of time.

He came to the conclusion not only that he was a worthless waster himself, an alcohol-dependent drug-addict, but also that he was the cause of everybody else's problems.

Look at the disappointment I have been to my parents, he thought. I have given them more bother and caused them more concern than all the rest of the family put together.

And look at the failure I have been for Linda, too. Linda who loves me so much, he thought. All I have brought her since the day I met her has been trouble and worry.

Now comes this, he thought. Our baby is going to die.

And it's my fault. All of it.

Chris couldn't face it. He was failing in the capacity to cope test.

As he lay there on his brother's bed, drinking a can of beer, he decided to end it all.

I will take the quick and easy way out, he thought.

There is no hope, no prospect, no future for me, he concluded.

I will give myself, and everybody else, a bit of rest and peace.

My wife, my baby, and my parents will all be better off without me. And all the rest of the world at large, who don't care a toss about me anyway, will never even miss me.

I will do it...

Rising from the bed he crossed the landing into his and Linda's bedroom and collected all the tablets of different sorts that he could find, mostly valium and anti-depressants, and there were quite a few of them. Being married, or indeed living in with his parents, hadn't cured his cravings.

Chris was still heavily addicted to dope.

Then with the potentially lethal cocktail of tablets in his hand, he made his way back to his brother's bedroom, where he had left what remained of his can of beer on the chest of drawers.

Sitting down again on the edge of the bed, Chris put his plan for the freedom of his friends into practice.

He didn't take one tablet. Or two. Or three.

Nor did he take one **sort** of tablet. Or two. Or three.

He took a handful of them, three or four at a time.

All washed down with short gulps of beer.

And there were all sorts of them.

All washed down with short gulps of beer.

To combine drugs and alcohol was always a dangerous thing to do, he had always been told. So surely this monster mixture he had taken should do the trick....

When he had downed every tablet Chris returned to his own bedroom. He felt desperately sick. Surely it must be going to work. And soon...

Linda had by that time come up into their bedroom, and was tidying up around. And preparing for bed.

When she saw the state of her husband she became alarmed, but not unusually so. His eyes were rolling in his head. He had turned a ghastly pale grey-green colour.

Then he attempted to speak to her. It was obvious he was trying to say something but couldn't find the words.

He collapsed in a limp lump on the floor.

Chris has been drinking again, Linda decided. And this was why she had not become overly excited, or panicked unduly. For Chris had drunk himself legless at least once a week since their wedding.

Linda ran downstairs to her mother-in-law who had been so kind to her. "I'm sorry to say I think Chris is drunk again," she began, almost apologetically. "Could we possibly get him downstairs on to the settee to sleep it off?" she wondered.

This procedure had become normal practice.

Downstairs on the big maroon settee was where Chris usually 'slept it off'.

Tommy Killen was called upon to help and between them the perplexed parents and the worried wife half carried, half trailed the dead-weight form of the unconscious Chris down the stairs and into the living room. And there they made him as comfortable as possible.

They made sure his head was to the side so that he wouldn't choke, if he was sick.

They placed a rug over him so that he wouldn't be cold, if he wakened.

And then they left him, to go to bed themselves.

He would be O.K. in the morning.

He had always been O.K. in the morning, before.

They hadn't the slightest clue, though, what Chris had just taken. They just assumed he was drunk.

But he wasn't.

Would he be, as they had presumed, 'O.K. in the morning'?!

9

A HOUSE, BUT NOT A HOME

At four o'clock in the morning May Killen awoke with a start. Her maternal instincts told her that Chris was very ill.

'Get an ambulance!' something seemed to say to her. 'Now! Immediately! At once!'

When she had pulled on a dressing-gown and tiptoed downstairs the anxious mother knew that she should do as intuition had instructed.

Chris lay just where and how they had left him. He looked deathly pale and was ominously motionless.

This wasn't a drunken stupor, she knew. Sadly she had seen some of them before.

Now there was no time to waste.

Rushing to the telephone May dialled 999 and summoned an ambulance. Then she dashed upstairs and when she had wakened her husband Tommy, and Linda, she told them of her strange awakening, her concern for Chris, and her urgent emergency call.

In twenty minutes time an ambulance arrived and as Chris was being carried out into it on a stretcher May Killen asked the question that was on all of their lips, "Will he be all right, do you think?"

"I don't know, dear," on of the paramedics replied, gently. "This looks pretty much like an overdose to me."

Chris was then taken to the Lagan Valley Hospital, in Lisburn, where he lay unconscious for three days, with medical staff battling to save his life.

This was most distressing for his young wife, the mother of their two week old infant.

Linda then found herself in the situation where her father-in-law Tommy was driving her the eight miles down into Belfast to visit her close-to-death daughter, and then bringing her back to Lisburn to visit her close-to-death husband.

Those were three days of nightmare. There was a sense of uncanny unreality about the whole thing. It was like living through a bad dream, when she never seemed to be able to waken up, shake it off, and walk away.

She had not yet fully recovered physically and emotionally from Samantha's premature birth. And now she was having to cope with all of this.

Linda was passing her capacity to cope test. With flying colours.

The kind words, practical deeds, and continued prayers of many genuinely concerned people, in addition to her ever-attentive in-laws, were a great source of comfort to her during those difficult days.

One such reassuring incident happened on Chris's second day in hospital. It was late afternoon before Linda arrived in the Lagan Valley, having already been to Belfast, where she had been heartened by the news from the Jubilee. Samantha was improving.

That was great. It was just one tiny chink of light in the constant sense of night that seemed to surround her at that time.

But what would she find in here?

Linda was walking along the corridor with an already lighter step when suddenly she was forced to make an emergency stop.

As she approached the downstairs ward where Chris was lying, Linda heard a voice which she was sure she had heard before.

Creeping forward slowly she peered round the curtain at the end of the four-bedded bay.

Yes. She had been right. She **had** recognized the voice. It was the voice of the Rev. Scott, who had married them the year before in St. Columba's Presbyterian Church. How could she ever forget that?!

This earnest minister was down on his knees at her husband's bedside, praying for him, out loud. He was pleading with God 'to spare this young man to his young wife and little child'. It didn't seem to matter to him that he was in the middle of a busy ward in the middle of a busy day. He knew he had to commit this whole serious situation into the hand of God, as a matter of urgency. And he was getting on with it.

Linda waited quietly, reverently, tearfully, until he had finished. She was impressed by his sincerity. And touched by his tenderness.

As he left the ward, bending forward to give his knees a quick swipe of a dust, the minister spotted the young wife and mother standing silently dabbing at her cheek with a paper tissue.

"Don't worry, Linda. I believe Chris will recover," he said to comfort her, trying to sound as confident as he could. "I have brought his case before the Lord. And we can only leave it in His hands. The doctors and nurses are doing all they possibly can for him. And God will do the rest."

Linda found his calm confidence most reassuring. Here was somebody else who believed in God. And in talking to Him in prayer.

Somebody, that was, as well as Aunt Violet.

It was just the previous night that Linda's mum had informed her that she had contacted Aunt Violet, told her the whole story, and asked her to pray for Chris. That God would spare his life.

That would not be a problem. Only a privilege, she had been told.

Aunt Violet had promised that she and her praying friends would make Chris and his condition a matter for special prayer.

Not only were Violet and her prayer-partners making Chris and his critical condition a focus of their fervent prayers, although that had present priority. They were also praying for his critical spiritual condition.

These committed Christian people were not only beseeching God to heal the young man's beleaguered body, but they were pleading with Him to save his endangered soul as well.

Chris didn't know anything about the consternation his condition was causing though. He didn't know anything about anything. For three whole days.

He was completely out of it. Dead to the world.

Then, on the fourth day there were positive signs.

The patient's eyelids began to flicker. And he began to stir in the bed.

Slowly but surely Chris was returning to the world of consciousness.

When he first managed to open his eyes he saw a blur beside the bed. The blur was speaking. It was talking to him, and all the time trying to hide the sense of excitement in its voice.

Chris identified the voice first. Then the features of the blur-by-the-bed.

It was his Aunt Elsie.

He tried to make some sensible response. But couldn't. The effort of thinking, organizing, and then articulating was just too much.

With a sigh he lapsed back into oblivion.

Over the next twelve hours, though, after a period of coming-and-going, Chris became fully aware of all that was going on around him and began to communicate with the hospital staff and his relieved family.

His recovery was a tribute both to medical attention and the power of persistent prayer.

Chris didn't quite see it that way, however.

He had tried to switch off his stay on this sad and sorry scene.

But he had pushed the wrong button.

Instead of STOP he had mistakenly pressed PAUSE.

Now his wife, his parents and a plethora of other praying people who had all wanted to see the rest of the programme had gone and pressed PLAY.

And here he was. Back up and running again. Whether he liked it or not.

Perhaps things would begin to improve. It was all he could hope for .

At first it looked as though that was going to be the case.

Six days after he had been admitted to hospital, and a day before his release, Linda arrived up to visit him with a smile on her face. And a letter in her hand.

"They have a house for us, Chris," she said, with some pleasure.

'They' were the Housing Executive, and the house they were being offered was on the Old Warren estate in Lisburn.

"That's good," Chris replied. Then, recognizing that he hadn't sounded sufficiently excited, he upped the enthusiasm and went on, "That's great , Linda. Really great!"

After a one week stay in hospital, in which he had spent three days unconscious, one day half-conscious, and three days fully conscious, Chris was deemed fit to leave the Lagan Valley.

Linda and he moved back in with Tommy and May Killen.

Then came more good news.

Baby Samantha was progressing favourably and should be well enough to leave hospital in a week's time, too.

Everybody who could worked as hard as they could to prepare the new house for the baby's homecoming, and when she was considered well enough to be discharged, the house was ready for her to move into with her parents.

All three of them were together as a unit, at last. On their own.

It should have been ideal. A happy-family situation.

But it wasn't.

They had a house.

But it was not a home.

For Chris still had problems. Big problems.

With his health. And with his habits.

He was out of hospital, but he was still unwell. And it was no wonder.

For he was spending every penny they had.

On drink. And on drugs...

10

A NEW MAN, IN TWO WEEKS?

Within six months of his discharge from the Lagan Valley after his unproductive overdose, and going to live in the new house in the Old Warren with Linda and baby Samantha, Chris began to lose weight.

At first nobody paid much notice. Chris had not been eating a particularly regular or nourishing diet, so nobody actually expected him to be going about all well-fleshed and rosy-cheeked. A daily cocktail of drink and drugs is not on the highly-recommended and just-must-have list in the best Healthy Eating handbooks.

However when he started to be continually sick Linda insisted that he seek medical help.

Doctors began a course of injections to try and help sharpen his appetite. And also help him digest what he had eaten.

It was no good. The injections didn't do anything for him.

Then Chris developed acute abdominal pain.

One night he was in such intense yelling-out agony that a doctor was called and he in turn summoned an ambulance.

Chris was admitted to Belvoir Park Hospital, on the outskirts of Belfast, to an isolation unit. He appeared to have all the symptoms of salmonella poisoning.

After two days treatment in that unit the patient's condition hadn't improved. It had rather become worse. Chris was very ill. And in agony.

Having been three days in Belvoir Park, Chris was transferred to Belfast's City Hospital for further investigation. And it was there, after further extensive tests, that his condition was eventually diagnosed.

Probably as a result of all the drugs he had taken in his tearaway teenage years the young patient's stomach and intestines were found to be in a terrible state. Multiple adhesions had occurred. Only surgery could sort him out.

For three more preparation-for-operation days Chris lay in hospital, seriously ill.

Linda visited her husband every day and there were times that she left the hospital wondering if she would see him the next day. How could he possibly survive the night? He was so very weak. And ill. And apathetic.

It was this emotionless listlessness that worried her most. Chris didn't seem to care about her, or Samantha, or anybody or anything she could tell him about any more. He didn't even seem to care whether he lived or died .

She knew that he had planned to take his life before, but now perhaps he was going to get his way. Fulful his desire. Realize his ambition. And die, leaving them all better off, as he had considered they would be, without him.

That wasn't what the junior house doctor seemed to think, though, when it came time for his operation.

As Chris was being prepared for the theatre the doctor tried to cheer him up, with a positive forecast of the possible outcome.

"Don't worry, Chris, once you have had this operation you will be out of here in two weeks," he predicted. And then to add emphasis to his optimism he went on, "And what's more, you will be a new man!"

It would be great if only that could be true.

Chris Killen would dearly love to be a new man. For he felt pretty much like an old man. Or no man at all, at the moment.

He was a physical wreck, a prodigal son, a hopeless husband and an absentee father. And he was also acutely aware that there was still something sadly missing in his life. The lack he had first felt in London hadn't gone away. Even though Linda, whom he at that time longed for, was now his wife. There was an emptiness within him which nothing he seemed to do, or take, or experience, could ever fill.

As part of his search for peace of mind and satisfaction of soul, Chris still carried his little burgundy Gideon Testament with him, everywhere he went. So it was not surprising that he had brought it with him into the hospital, and stowed it away in his locker.

Late at night, or early in the morning, when the ward was quiet, and if he was physically able, Chris slipped it out. Sometimes he read quite a bit, sometimes he was only able to read a few verses before he felt waves of nausea sweeping over him, and sometimes he discovered that he was so sick and dizzy that he couldn't read at all. On those occasions even holding it in his hand was a comfort. It was an old familiar friend, he felt. And he reasoned, possibly somewhat naively, that perhaps having it and merely holding it would somehow keep God on his side.

During the times when he was well enough to concentrate, Chris read isolated unconnected portions, mostly in the Gospels. He liked to read about Jesus. It was soothing somehow.

Indeed he was later to discover that in those days of intense physical and mental anguish he had actually underlined some verses. These were verses which he had first learnt as a child in Great Victoria Street Baptist Church Sunday School, and had recognized, all those years later. However, he had no recollection of ever underlining them. But he had done it. Himself. In agony. In hospital.

By concentrating largely on reading in the Gospels, Chris hadn't as yet discovered what his New Testament had to say about the making of a new man. When Paul was writing to some Christians in Corinth he told them that 'if any man was in Christ he was a new creation'. In effect, he was a new man. Everything old had vanished and a totally new created being had emerged. Like a beautiful butterfly bursting forth from a chrysalis.

Chris hadn't found that verse, or experienced the wonder of that transforming experience. Yet.

He was still searching ,though.

Aunt Violet hadn't given up on praying for him yet, either.

And the hospital staff had promised they would make a new man of him, physically, at least.

In two weeks.

That would always be a start!

11

WHAT A REVOLTING MESS!

After his surgery Chris was soon up and about. It seemed as though it had all worked out as forecast. He felt so much better, and would soon be home, a whole new man. That would be wonderful, and such a change.

Then things took a dramatic turn for the worse.

It was exactly two weeks after his operation and almost six o'clock on a Monday morning. All was still in Ward 2 South.

Chris woke up with a start in his dimly-lit side ward.

He was overcome with a deep sense of foreboding. Something had gone horribly wrong. He could feel it in his bones. Or perhaps it was his body.

Putting his hand down the bed he felt something warm and sticky. His bed seemed to be saturated in this stuff, whatever it was. On drawing his hand out from under the sheets he found that it was covered with reddish blackish congealing blood.

His fingers were stuck together.

And his heart was struck with terror.

Lifting up the bedcovers to peer nervously below Chris discovered that he was lying in a veritable pool of his own blood. And this wasn't just ordinary blood, either. It seemed to be laced with big lumps and clumps of slimy stuff.

What a revolting mess!

The petrified patient panicked.

He yelled and shouted and pressed his buzzer all at once.

A nurse, sensing the urgency in his hysterical scream, and hearing his buzzer being sounded so insistently, rushed into the ward.

"Help me nurse! Help me! I am bleeding badly!" Chris howled in desperation.

The duty nurse took one look at the blood-bath-bed and dashed back out again, even faster than she had come in. Then a house doctor arrived in the side-ward, white coat flying.

Soon the bed was surrounded. The consultant who had performed the original operation had been summoned and he hastily arranged for major emergency surgery.

The immediate concern of the medical staff was to save the young father's life. He was haemorrhaging badly from his wound. The blood was pouring from his body.

Nurses with needles prodded for a vein in each arm and two lines of blood were put in. This was to establish a potentially life-saving transfusion until the root cause of the problem could be corrected on the operating-table.

Chris was rushed to the theatre for that surgery. The entire surgical team knew that they were in a frantic race against time to save this man's life.

So urgent was this case that there was no time for the customary pre-operation preparation.. Chris was wheeled straight into the theatre and lay looking up at the big powerful lights, which were shining down on him.

Am I going to die? he wondered. He felt so faint, though, that he didn't even feel frightened. The surgeons would do their best, he knew, and he was overcome with a strange resignation to the inevitable. It was fatalism without fear.

As they were preparing to perform the operation the two surgeons who had come together in an attempt to stem the bleeding and save his life told Chris what they suspected had happened. The original surgery had all come apart. His inside organs had all been in such a shocking state to start with that all the original work had proved in vain. It hadn't held together.

The situation, as they explained it to their patient, reminded Chris of some verses he had read in his little New Testament once. They were all something about the futility of pouring new wine into old wineskins, and the stupidity of trying to use strong fresh thread to stitch up an old and well-worn garment. In that kind of scenario things didn't usually improve. They just got worse.

The surgeons weren't prepared to give up on Chris, though.

They were going to give it another try, they told him. They were going to make an all out effort to repair the damage, control the flow of blood, and then put him all together again. For good, and for ever, they hoped.

It was the only course of action open to them, and they only hoped that it would work. But it was all a race against time...

Meanwhile back in Lisburn, Tommy Killen had been phoned by the hospital to say that Chris was critically ill and had been rushed to the theatre. He immediately set off to his sick son's house to alert his sick son's wife. Chris and Linda didn't have a telephone at that time, so mum and dad Killen were their point of contact with the hospital, and indeed many others agencies also.

May Killen undertook to care for baby Samantha while wife and father set off for Belfast City Hospital, not knowing what to expect.

On arriving up in Ward 2 South Tommy and Linda were informed that Chris was still in the theatre. And that it was just 'touch and go' whether or not he would pull through, since he had lost so much blood. He was, they said, dangerously ill.

What a day that was. Anxious father and anxious wife sat together in the tiny waiting room in the hospital. They spoke to each other only when they could think of anything remotely relevant to say, but mostly they sat in silence, staring blankly at the wall. Linda reckoned she had worked out every shade in the pattern in the curtain on the window and identified every mark on the floor by the end of the second hour. And still they were there.

Although they were only waiting for hours and hours and hours it seemed much longer. More like days and days and days. Tommy looked at his watch over and over again, and when he thought that at least forty minutes must have passed he found that it was only four!

Every time a doctor or senior nurse came along the corridor they were on the edges of their seats, ready to rise to meet them, and take the bad news as bravely as possible

None of them ever came into their little room though, and Tommy and Linda looked at each other with a relieved sigh, when the possibility of an interview was past. No news could only be good news, they had come to conclude

And so the day progressed.

It was well on into the afternoon when Tommy and Linda were given the news, and by that time they had prepared themselves for the worst. The news was however that the worst hadn't happened.

The surgeons had been able to repeat their former operation, more successfully they believed, and Chris had survived. So far, so good.

When they were admitted to the Intensive Care ward to see him later on that evening wife and father were both relieved and shocked.

They were relieved that Chris was still alive at all, but shocked at his physical state. It was obvious that he was still gravely ill, and that his continued survival was dependent on the complicated array of hardware all around him. And the power of prayer.

The pale figure in the bed was hooked up to all sorts of drips and drains, tubes and monitors. And back in Dromara Aunt Violet and her prayer partners were back on red alert, bearing the desperately ill Chris up before their God in earnest prayer.

Everyone was pleased that Chris had pulled through yet another crisis, but there was still a long, long, way to go.

He wasn't quite the new man he had expected to be, just yet.

And wouldn't be for another day or two either it seemed!

12

A REAL NIGHTMARE

For days Chris hovered between life and death. His condition had been grave. His operation had been major. So his chances of recovery had been rated at no more than 'fifty-fifty'.

Twice every day Linda and her father-in-law, Tommy, came up to see him. Chris was kept in the Intensive Care ward for a week. It was distressing for the young wife and mother, and for his patient, anxious parents.

Eight days after his life-saving emergency surgery Chris was deemed well enough to go back to the normal ward, and so he returned to the familiar surroundings of Ward 2 South.

Recovery was a slow, and painful process. Over the previous month, and during his stay in hospital Chris had lost three stones in weight and as a result of all the operations and medication he was pitifully weak. After he had been confined to bed for almost four weeks it was time for Chris to put his feet to the floor once more.

And it was almost like learning to walk all over again! Indeed for months after that he could only walk with the help of a stick or other walking aid. Chris Killen, not long turned twenty, looked like a man of ninety, shuffling about the hospital.

As he began to find his feet again, and as he slowly regained strength, Chris occasionally became depressed by the apparently pointless and seemingly endless monotony of the hospital routine. He hated being confined by the physical limitations of his ward, for he was never allowed to go out beyond its door. The fact that he was totally dependent on pain-killing drugs for any sort of comfort ever, annoyed him as well.

Would he ever be able to walk outside and spend time with Linda and nurse little Samantha, like any normal husband and father? he wondered.

Would he ever be free from the excruciating pain that often bent him double in agony? he wondered.

There were times when he pondered the point of everything. Or anything, for that matter.

If they had just let me die when I tried to finish it all, he mused in deepest gloom, then everybody, and not least myself, would have been spared all this agony and misery.

It was a nightmare.

There were lighter moments when the occasional light-hearted banter on the ward lifted his spirits, but for most of the time, and especially in the stillness of the night, Chris found himself enveloped in a sense of mental desolation. The hospital staff must have recognized their long-term patient's recurring lapses into melancholy for they demonstrated one day that they were keeping him under constant surveillance.

Chris was standing at the window, gazing out, his face set in a fixed looking-but-not-seeing expression. He was leaning forward with both hands resting on the glass above his head in the I-surrender-shoot-me-now position.

Suddenly a nurse and an orderly seemed to appear out of nowhere, one at either side of him, and grabbed him by the upraised arms. They knew that it would be virtually impossible for anyone to break the reinforced glass and take a jump from there, but they also knew the past history of their patient. Their records showed that Chris had attempted suicide before. And crazy people try crazy things, sometimes.

Ten weeks after he had been admitted to hospital for his new-man-in-two-weeks treatment, Chris was eventually allowed to go home. Although he was out of Ward 2 and back into the Old Warren, he hadn't been cleared from hospital treatment, however.

His wasn't the 'you can go home, here are your pills, see your own G P, and we will send you a card to come back in six months', sort of discharge.

Chris was still so weak and in so much pain that he had to return to the hospital every night for four months for a change of dressing and a morphine injection.

During the next three years Chris Killen lived a life of pain. Of fear. And then of terrifying nightmares.

After his every-night-of-the-week-for-four-months-for-treatment visits to the hospital, Chris returned once every two weeks for further specialist care, which often involved yet more corrective surgery. Hospitalization became so much part of his life that Chris stopped counting after his twenty-eighth operation. Each of these courses of treatment involved an overnight or perhaps two-night stopover in Ward 2 South.

In these frequent visits to hospital Chris invariably had his little red Gideon New Testament with him. He didn't always read it, but he always had it, for he felt safer with it somehow. And anyway, he might need it some day.

His little daughter Samantha was growing up rapidly. From a bouncing baby she had become an inquisitive toddler and then on through to a charming three year old, but her daddy had hardly noticed.

Her father had been so busy trying to keep himself alive, and endeavouring to make himself happy, that he virtually missed his little daughter's early and interesting years. The burden of raising their child, and entertaining her husband's drinking cronies fell upon the often-hard-pressed wife and mother, Linda.

Often on a Saturday night some of their friends and relatives would come around to their house, carrying their quota of cans, for a big booze-up. This was not, as one could imagine, ideal for Chris's health, but he mistakenly thought that it was good for his happiness.

Having had so many operations, Chris was in practically unending, practically unbearable, pain. There were times, too, when he had a peculiar sensation that he was about to have another horrendous haemorrhage. More than once he sent Linda packing off down to the nearest phone box, in the middle of the night, to phone his dad, to ask him to come at once to take him to the City Hospital. And every single time when they got there it was discovered to be a false alarm.

Having had one such chilling experience, Chris was beset by constant fear of a repeat performance.

Then a further, and even more distressing, complication began to manifest itself.

Chris had been given so much morphine, legally, for the relief of his constant pain, that he had become addicted to the opiate-based drug.

One of the side-effects of this addiction was that he began to have horrifying nightmares. Linda would be awakened by her husband shouting out in terror, perspiration rolling from his body.

The nightmares all had the same sort of theme. They were of being trapped in shocking situations with no possible means of escape. Impending and horrific death seemed to be the inevitable outcome of every ordeal. Chris always tried frantically to wake up, but felt that he couldn't.

The torment just rolled on and on.

These nightmares soon became so frequent, and so frightening that Chris often found himself weak and exhausted, but afraid to fall asleep. It would be better to stay awake all night than to endure another unnerving nightmare.

With indefinite hospital treatment stretching out ahead of him, as far as the mind could see, but with no prospect of ever being any better, with perpetual insufferable pain, and now with these horrific nightmares, life had become almost intolerable for Chris, again.

Life had become a real nightmare, either at night or by day.

Would it, or could it, possibly go on like this?

13

CONSIDER YOUR OPTIONS

In late July, 1989, the consultant who had seen Chris so many times, and had operated on him so often, became concerned that his patient didn't appear to be making any appreciable progress. With this in mind he invited Chris and Linda to meet him to consider their options.

When the young couple went to the City Hospital to keep their appointment, the consultant explained to them that he couldn't continue treating Chris as he had been doing, indefinitely. He realized that the treatment had proved to be merely a holding-for-the-present rather than a healing-for-the-future exercise.

He went on to tell them that he felt there was something more which could be done. A specialist in Chris's particular complaint could be brought in to perform very major surgery. There would be, he cautioned, a more-than-usual risk with this eight-hour operation but he felt that it would end the succession of minor, but patently ineffective, monthly-or-more visits to his clinic.

Chris and Linda were invited to consider this carefully as an option.

The choice was stark.

Chris could decide to undergo the surgery, which could go either way. It could leave him able to live the normal life he had always craved. Or it could leave Linda a widow, and Samantha fatherless. It was as serious as that.

The alternative to the operation was just to continue as they had been doing. The pain. The morphine. And the ever more terrifying nightmares.

Having given it due consideration Chris and Linda concluded that they should ask the consultant to arrange for the potentially transforming surgery to be carried out. They reckoned that it was worth the risk for Chris felt that there was no way he could carry on in his present condition much longer. He was by then a physical and mental wreck and the strain of it all certainly wasn't improving the quality of their married life.

On having been informed of their decision the consultant arranged for the operation to proceed.

Chris was to be admitted to Belfast City Hospital on Sunday 13th August in preparation for surgery on Tuesday 15th.

All went according to the prearranged plan and Chris was very ill, and in the Intensive Care Ward for some days after the operation. Again Linda and Tommy visited faithfully twice daily, and sat watching Chris battle for life.

Within a week his condition had shown a marked improvement. The danger was over. The risk had been worth taking, and surely Chris would be a new man this time.

No more needles. And no more nightmares. It seemed almost too good to be true, somehow.

Friday, 25th August was to be a day of good news, and a fond farewell for Chris.

The good news came when his consultant made his ward round that morning.

"You have come on well Chris," he told the much improved patient, "and we are going to keep you in here over the weekend to keep an eye on you. If you continue to make progress in the way that you have been doing I see no reason why you shouldn't go home on Monday."

That was marvellous. Since he felt better than he had ever done over the previous three or four years, Chris looked forward to being at home and being a normal person, doing normal things.

The other piece of information that the consultant gave Chris caused him to hastily blink away a hastily formed tear. For the senior doctor was leaving the hospital too, but not to go home and convalesce. He was retiring, after a lifetime of service in the medical profession, and was looking forward to doing all sorts of things he had missed out on during a very busy career.

Chris was sad at that, for he had been so good to, and long-suffering with him. He had long since lost count of the number of times this man had cut him open, sorted him out, and stitched him up. It must have been dozens!

When he spoke to some of the nurses about the that-night departure of such a senior figure in the Hospital, they invited Chris to the retirement party up in a speedily adapted staff common room.

They didn't seem to consider it unusual to invite a patient to such a party, for the patient had been in their ward so often that they looked upon him as one of themselves. A part of the furniture. When asking him if he would like to come to the retirement presentation one of the staff recalled how Chris had made them laugh more than a year previously when he had announced, "I am creating a record here today!"

"How do you mean?" some of them had enquired, puzzled.

"I have now lain in every single bed in Ward 2 South!" was what he told them.

So Chris went to the party.

A cake had been baked for the occasion, a retirement gift had been bought, glowing tributes had been prepared and practised, and genuine smiles through genuine tears were expected.

Up in the common room Chris enjoyed the farewell party.

He ate his slice of cake, clapped at the presentation, laughed heartily or nodded seriously, as appropriate, during the speeches, and smiled his genuine smiles through his genuine tears, with all the rest.

It had been a good night, but as he climbed into bed to pass another night before he, too, left the hospital, hopefully for good, Chris felt funny. Sort of sick.

Lying there, staring at the ceiling, he attempted to convince himself that it had been either the unusual excitement or the unaccustomed indulgence of the retirement party that had knocked him out of sorts.

He would be fine in the morning.

And then it would only be two days until he was home.

A new man at last!

14

THERE IS A WAY

Chris had hoped to be fine in the morning.

Chris had expected to be fine in the morning. And for many, many mornings to come.

That was not to be, however.

As had happened so many times in this very ill young man's very tortuous last three years, his condition took a dramatic downturn. All of a sudden.

He had been right. He had felt queasy. And it hadn't been the party, or the cake that had caused it, either.

In the early hours of Saturday morning Chris began to be persistently, and violently sick. He just couldn't stop vomiting. His stomach had become hard, and swollen. Like an over-pumped football. It was terribly sore, too. Very tender to the touch.

In a crazed combination of impetuous panic and intense pain Chris pressed his buzzer fiercely. He simply stuck his thumb on it, and kept it there.

Then it all began, all over again. The same old routine that had become a feature of this young husband's struggle for survival.

The duty nurse took one look at him, and immediately called the house doctor.

The houseman examined him and immediately called the senior house officer.

Although very ill Chris was reassured when this senior house officer appeared at his bedside. He felt he knew him very well, for he had been in charge of his case on his early visits to the City Hospital, more than three years previously. For at least a year he hadn't been around, but obviously now he was back.

Familiarity in this case had fostered friendship. Chris knew this senior medical man by his Christian name. To him he was Robert.

The screens had been hastily drawn around the bed and for the next half-an-hour there was a seemingly ceaseless scurrying to and fro. Nurses came and went, fetching stands, tubes, needles, drips and drugs. All the usual paraphernalia. The two doctors gave brief but urgent instructions.

In that pressurized position everyone was working flat out to keep Chris Killen alive. For yet another time.

When all the bustle had abated and all the lines were in and all the drips were up Chris felt he was back to square one. He had been here before, somehow. More than once. It was as though he hadn't received one single course of treatment even with all his comings and goings to hospitals.

So much for the high-risk eight-hour operation, he thought.

He certainly wasn't a new man, yet. Nor would he be, for a while, he reckoned.

As these thoughts tumbled around in his tormented mind a strange, cold, feeling of fear began to overwhelm the panicking patient. Having been granted temporary respite from the terrible pain and horrible nausea, the sheer gravity and stark reality of his situation struck him like a hammer blow, for the very first time. This had never happened to him before through all his previous touch-and-go experiences.

'I am going to die this time,' he thought, in terror. 'Surely I can't make it out of this one. They cannot possibly save my life again. My body is in an absolute mess. How could the doctors, no matter how clever they are , save me now? Or ever?'

When they were eventually on their own in the confined space behind the screens, the senior house officer sat down on the edge of his patient's bed.

"I am afraid we are going to have to take you down to the theatre right away, Chris," he broke the news gently. "Your insides are in a bad way. You have adhesions again."

Struggling valiantly to keep his surging emotions under control, and be the big-brave-boy he had managed to be so often before, Chris asked, "Tell me honestly, Robert, how ill am I?"

That was a hard question for the S.H.O.. But an honest response had been requested, and an honest response, he had always found, was best in the end.

"You are very, very seriously ill, Chris," he replied, softly.

On hearing that, an inexplicable sense of impending doom overcame the man in the bed. A big black shadow had descended upon him, blocking out all light. And any slim shaft of hope. The doctor's diagnosis just confirmed to him what he thought he already knew. It merely served to substantiate the patently obvious.

'I am going to die tonight,' he was convinced. 'I know it. I can feel it. And I am not ready to meet God. That is my big, big problem. If I don't survive this operation, I will be in hell. There can be no doubt about that after the life I have lived.'

Then he turned, in the fertile flow of his anguished mind, to all those who through their lives, and by their words had warned him about the realities of life and death, of heaven and hell, about the punishment for sin and the love of God...

There had been his mother, then the kind lady who had taken him to Sunday School in the Baptist Church when he had been just a boy, years ago, and Aunt Violet. All these people seemed so sure of themselves. So confident in their salvation. So certain they would be in heaven when they died.

And every single one of them had assured him, often, that they were praying for him.

Chris began to sob softly. He couldn't help himself. The big-brave-boy and the hard-man-skinhead image had both gone. Vanished into thin air. Evaporated in the increasing heat of an imminent hell.

The prodigal son, the drug-taking rebel, the drunken husband and failing father was broken. Shattered. Convicted. And scared to death, of death.

Robert, who was not only a dedicated doctor, but also a committed Christian, noticed that Chris was visibly upset. He sensed, too, that this emotional disturbance stemmed from something other, something deeper, than merely his perplexing physical plight.

"What's wrong, Chris?" he enquired, sympathetically, in an effort to afford the troubled young man an opportunity to personally express his conspicuous concerns. "Are you worried about the surgery?"

"No, it's not the operation that's worrying me, Robert. Sure I have had dozens of them before," Chris replied through his tears.

Then, after a brief pause to recompose himself, he blurted out the real reason for his evident distress.

"I am afraid I am going to die, and that's what wrong with me, Robert," he confessed candidly, at last. "And I am afraid to die because I am not prepared to die.
I am terrified of dying because I have lived a wild, godless life, and now I am afraid of death, and God, and judgment, and hell..."

Robert sat in silence for a few minutes. He now had the full picture. Chris had torn open his already-breaking heart, and exposed his anguished soul before him.

The Christian doctor was glad, at that moment, that his own personal experience extended beyond his medical qualifications. He knew he had the answer to this patient's pressing need.

Looking directly into his miserable, tear-strewn face, Robert said to the anxious young man, "You know Chris there is a way that you can be prepared for death. People who have trusted in Christ as their Saviour don't fear death like a lot of other people do."

Chris nodded at that. He had just been thinking of some of them earlier.

Then, leaning forward, Robert picked up Chris's ever present burgundy Gideon New Testament from its prominent position on the locker.

"Do you mind if I read a verse or two to you from your little Testament?" he asked.

"No. I don't mind at all. Please do," Chris invited, glad of the company of such a caring Christian at such a critical time.

"Remember I told you that there **is** a way in which you can be prepared for death, and also to be sure of going to heaven after death," the S.H.O. went on, leafing purposefully through the little red book in his hand. "Listen to this..."

As Chris sat listening intently, Robert began to read, "Jesus saith unto him, I am the way, the truth and the life : no man cometh unto the Father, but by me."

Closing the book with his finger in the place, Robert continued, "Hear that, Chris? There **is** a way. Jesus is not only **a** way, but He said Himself that He is THE Way."

Confident that he had his patient's undivided attention, and that this message was exactly what he needed at that moment, the doctor read another verse, but it was one which Chris already knew. He had remembered it from the Baptist Sunday School.

It was John chapter three, and verse sixteen, "For God so loved the world, that he gave his only begotten Son, that whosoever believeth in him should not perish, but have everlasting life."

This verse was followed in quick succession, just as quickly as Robert could find them, by a number of others, which Chris didn't instantly recognize. One of them said that 'Christ hath once suffered for sins, the just for the unjust to bring us to God', and another stated that 'There is therefore now no condemnation to them that are in Christ Jesus.'

When satisfied that he had read enough verses from the New Testament to illustrate his point, Robert closed it and replaced it on the locker. Then, with Chris lying back on his prop-me-up pillows, he explained as simply as he could the way of salvation, how that Jesus Christ had come into the world with one express purpose in view. He had come, Robert said, to die on the cross to take away the punishment that we deserved for the sins that we had committed. If we confessed our sins and trusted in Christ then we would be saved. And when we are saved we have no need to fear death, or what lies beyond death, because Jesus promised His disciples that He was going to prepare a place, called heaven, for them. It was at that time, too, that He told them that He was the Way, and the only Way, to it.

It became clear from the sounds outside the screens, that Chris was soon going to be wheeled away to the theatre. Robert knew that there wasn't much time left.

"Would you like to be saved, Chris?" he asked, with the warmth of a concerned counsellor.

"Yes, I would like to be saved. And I want to be saved NOW," came the honest, earnest, reply.

"O.K. then, Chris," the senior doctor said, "I am going to pray with you and for you. As I do so you can bow your head and quietly confess you sins to God, and ask Him to save you."

With that, and not wanting to waste any further time, he began to pray. With Chris, and for him, as he had promised.

It was while he was praying, too, that Chris did as his friend had suggested. He confessed his sins to God, and acknowledging that Jesus had died on the cross to save him from the penalty of those very sins, asked Him to come into his heart, and to be his Saviour.

And the wonderful thing was that He did. There and then.

Chris was saved. And he knew it!

So did Robert, too, when he opened his eyes.

The critically-ill Chris was smiling through his tears.

He had just reached out his hand to shake Robert's and was in the process of exclaiming, "Thank you Robert, thank you! I have just got saved! Thank you! Thank you!" when a porter poked his head around the screens.

"Excuse me sir," he began, addressing the senior house officer, "we have come to take this patient to theatre."

Chris waved weakly to Robert as he was wheeled away.

At least now he wasn't scared to die any more.

He was prepared for death, or life, or anything else.

'There **is** a way,' his friend had told him.

As the porters swung his trolley into the theatre he was so glad that he had found it!

15

CAN YOU PROVE IT?

Just after Chris had gone into the theatre, with a sense of peace in his soul, the phone rang in his home in Lisburn.

It was someone from the hospital to let Linda know that the husband she had seen survive so many life-or-death situations was in yet another one. He had been 'taken to the theatre again', she was informed.

Linda immediately began to phone around. She called Tommy and May Killen, her father- and mother-in-law, and broke the news to them. They instantly volunteered to take her down to 'The City' straight away, and after the young mother had arranged for someone to look after her baby, Samantha, they left.

On arriving at the hospital they went to the ward, and from there were directed to the operating-theatre where the surgeons were battling to make 'a new man' of Chris, physically, another time. No one but God, his new Heavenly Father, and Robert, his doctor, counsellor and friend, knew that he had already become 'a new creation in Christ Jesus', spiritually, just a few hours before.

It was early on Saturday morning. The hospital was just beginning to stir into life after another night of muted activity. Nursing shifts were changing. From far away down some distant corridor breakfast trolleys were rattling and clattering. Another day had begun.

Most of this rising din of daily routine seemed completely removed from the virtual-reality of the world of Linda, May and Tommy. It was as though it was all happening on some distant planet, millions of miles from earth.

Linda was so anxious, and so agitated, that she couldn't ever settle herself long enough to sit down. Her in-laws' repeated question, "Will you not sit down here a minute, Linda, and take the weight off your legs?", went unheeded. Their daughter-in-law didn't intend to be rude. She just couldn't feel the weight on her legs for the weight on her mind.

When she was not pacing up and down in short bursts Linda was standing staring blankly at the theatre door, wondering when it was going to open. And what the message would be when it did.

It was only when she stopped and stood, body still but mind awhirl, that she realized that there was somebody else parading about. It was the security man. Up and down the corridor he padded, up and down, up and down, speaking cheerily to staff as they passed and nodding knowingly to the troubled trio, outside the theatre door.

Tommy and May sat speechless for most of the time. It was one of those occasions when it was hard to find anything sensible or significant to say. So they sat side by side on the chairs in the corridor, each deriving solace from the company of the other. Father Tommy spent the most of his morning gazing at his own specially selected square yard of the opposite wall, while mother May seemed to spend at least some of her time with her head bowed. She was praying so hard, as she had done so often before, for her so wayward, and now so weak, son Chris.

After what seemed like hours, the door that Linda had been studying so intently for so long was pulled open.

A surgeon whom she recognized, for he had operated on Chris before, came across to her.

"You will be glad to know your husband seems to have pulled through again, Mrs. Killen," he said with a weary man's wan smile of I'm-glad-that's-over satisfaction.

Then, noticing Linda's deep sigh of relief, he went on, "Would you like to go in and see him for a minute? He is in the recovery room."

"Yes, please. Just for a minute, as you say, if that would be possible," Linda replied, her hand already reaching out to grab the door.

Linda had seen her Chris in a critical condition often, but she was momentarily taken aback when she saw him in the recovery room that morning. There were drips and drains attached to almost every visible part of his body. There were stands on either side of the trolley he was lying on, and tubes above it, beside it, below it. Everywhere. It was frightening.

Perhaps the most perplexing thing of all to the worried wife, because she had never seen him so soon after an operation before, was that he was covered in a type of tinfoil stuff. She wasn't quite sure whether he looked like a shot-up-shot-down casualty from some outer space odyssey, or a turkey, plucked and stuffed and ready for the oven. But she hated the image of either.

As she tiptoed over to stand beside him, Chris was in the very early stages of the return to reality. His eyelids were flickering, and he was drifting in and out of consciousness. At that stage, though, he was more out than in.

Once, when he was able to focus sufficiently to determine that the person standing beside him wasn't either a nurse, a doctor or an anesthetist, but his wife, Linda, he spoke to her. The last thing in his mind before being put to sleep prior to his operation, was obviously the first thing on his mind when he came round.

"Linda, I have got saved," he whispered, his voice cracked and dry.

"That's good, Chris. That's good," his wife replied, more to let him know that she had heard him than to express delight at what he had said. "Your operation is over now, and you are soon going to be well again," she went on, matching his whisper with hers. "Don't try to talk too much. Just rest. I will see you out on the ward later on."

Her last words had fallen on deaf ears. Chris was hearing nothing. He had lapsed back into oblivion.

As she walked out to rejoin her husband's still very concerned, if even a little consoled, parents, Linda answered their first instinctive question, "Well, how is he?", with an, "Oh, I think he will be O.K. He is still coming and going a bit but I'm sure he will be all right."

Deep in her heart, though, she was pondering what it was that Chris had been so keen to tell her.

He had said, 'I have got saved.'

As far as she was concerned that was going to take some believing

During the drive home to Lisburn, Linda dismissed that confession of faith in Christ as a mere passing fancy. It would last for a week, or possibly two at the most. A lot of people turn to religion in the face of death, she told herself. It's a sort of an any-port-in-a-storm, oh-God-please-help-me now reaction.

When she reflected on the life he had lived, and she knew more about it than anyone, for she had lived through some of it with him, Linda concluded that she would take some convincing.

What was he going to do about his dependence on drugs? Or the drunken parties, every weekend? There was hardly ever any room for food in their fridge. It was always packed full of cans and bottles of booze.

Then there was the swearing. What about it? Her husband had the most comprehensive vocabulary of profanities she had ever heard amongst all the folk she had ever met. And he wasn't afraid to use it, either. At any time. Or to anybody.

Time will tell, she told herself, but if Chris really has 'got saved', as he claims, then he will have to prove it. To me first, and then to hundreds of others after that.

And that was going to take some doing!

For it was going to mean a complete about turn, absolute, total and entire, in his whole of manner life!

16

'CONFESS WITH YOUR MOUTH'

At seven o'clock in the evening Tommy and May Killen took Linda back into the hospital to see Chris. This was to be the parents first time to see their son after his operation. Linda had already had that two-minute visit to her husband in the recovery room but as yet she hadn't told anyone about what he had said. In fact during that Saturday, with Samantha to care for, and enquiring telephone calls to answer, she had tried not to allow her mind to dwell too much upon it. To her it was just too far beyond the bounds of belief to even consider. And to tell anybody else about it would undoubtedly lead to red-faced retractions later on when Chris reverted to the drink, the drugs and the continual cursing.

That evening, however, Linda began to change her mind.

Although critically ill, only twelve hours after life-saving surgery, and still all wired up to all sorts of medical gadgetry, she observed a peace about her husband she had never seen before. He was more settled somehow. There was something too about the serene way he smiled at them all that told his wondering wife that he was definitely different, and that for the better. It was something she couldn't quite define, but she couldn't quite deny, either.

The big change that Linda noticed, and possibly his parents noticed too, was not only in the way he looked, but also in the way he said the few things he was able to say. After an operation like he had just undergone earlier that day he was understandably weak, but when he did summon up the strength to communicate at all, it was in a calm, controlled and confident manner.

He was just so thankful that his life had been spared. And he told them so, without an oath of any sort!

To Linda this was simply amazing.! Since she had met him, and even more so since she had married him, she had never known Chris to be able to describe anything, but especially sickness, pain and suffering, of which he had seemed to have more that his fair share, without an explosion of expletives.

Now he was telling them that he felt sick, and that he was very stiff and sore in different parts of his stitched-up abdomen. And the incredible thing was that he was managing to do it without using a single swear word. Not one! Not possible!

In himself, too, Chris felt that something definite had taken place. He felt so assured. So at peace. So prepared for whatever was to come, including death, if it should come to that.

A gnawing doubt kept him back from saying anything about it that Saturday evening, though.

'What if it isn't real?' it kept asking.

'What if you can't keep it?' it kept persisting.

'Are you not going to look one prize idiot if you tell them all you are a Christian and then you are back on the booze in a couple of weeks?' it kept taunting.

So the fears Linda had been entertaining about the possibility of the reality of her husband's conversion were also being experienced by Chris himself. He felt he was 'a new man in Christ Jesus' but he was scared to let anybody other than Linda know, in case the doubts that were besieging his brain turned out to be true.

And neither of them was saying anything more to each other about the claim that Chris had 'got saved last night'. Nor were they saying anything to anybody else, just yet.

The only spoken hint Chris gave that evening that something dramatic had happened in his life, and only Linda was able to interpret the significance of the request, came as they were leaving the ward.

As they were saying their 'Good-byes', one of a number of requests Chris made of his wife, who had a lot to remember, was to do with their cherished friend 'from up the country'.

"Could you give Aunt Violet a ring when you go home , Linda, and see if she would like to come up with you tomorrow afternoon?" he wondered. "I would like to see her."

When Linda phoned Aunt Violet, as they knew her, later that evening, she said she was free on the Sunday afternoon, and would be 'delighted' to go up and visit Chris.

Next day the busy wife and mother collected her great-aunt and brought her down to the City Hospital. The modest country lady could drive her Morris Minor at sometimes maddeningly moderate speeds along the rural roads around Dromara with almost total confidence, but she had never before driven to 'the city'. 'I would never dare to try to drive in Belfast,' she had told others often.

Chris had promised himself, lying quietly in bed that Sunday morning, that if Aunt Violet came up to the hospital that day, he was going to tell her, and anybody and everybody else who just happened to be there at the time, that he was saved. He had never read the verse in his little New Testament about 'confessing with your mouth the Lord Jesus', but he was going to do it, anyway. He had by then come to the stage that his newly-found faith had begun to mean so much to him that he wanted to tell everybody about it. And it was important to him that Aunt Violet should be one of the first to hear his good news. He was certain she would be pleased.

Although still physically extremely weak he was spiritually much stronger than he had been the night before. And he was sure the sense of settled satisfaction which he felt in his soul could only have been the result of his Friday night experience.

With his father and mother, Aunt Violet and Linda all standing around, Chris, still looking a pale and pathetic figure, lying flat in the bed, said, "I have something I would like to tell you all. I want you to know that I got saved on Friday night before my operation, and I have had a great sense of peace since."

As the audience around the bed listened with rapt attention, Chris recounted to them how he had been so terrified of death on Friday night, and how that Robert had read with him, prayed with him, and pointed him to faith in Christ.

Long before he had finished all he had to say, both May Killen, the mother who had loved him and prayed for him since the day he was born, and Aunt Violet, who had assured him she would 'be praying for him', from that first afternoon they had met up at her cottage in the country, were both weeping silently, but unashamedly. Tears of joy trickled slowly down their flushed cheeks.

When a satisfied smile on his lips had signalled the end of the 'confession of his mouth', Aunt Violet took a step forward and held the hand that lay limp across the top of the bedclothes.

"Chris, this is a wonderful answer to prayer!" she assured the now spiritually elated but physically exhausted man-in-the-bed.

"A lot of people have been praying for you in our wee fellowship. They will every one be delighted to hear this news!" she went on to inform him, the solemn nod of the head and the shining tears on the cheek convincing Chris that she meant every word of it.

"Thank you, Violet! Thank you!" Chris croaked hoarsely by way of reply, his voice breaking.

Linda noticed that the tears had begun to well up in his eyes, too.

NOW she was convinced about Chris, though still not a Christian herself.

And Aunt Violet had been praying for her for years!

Long before she had ever met him!

17

PRAISE THE LORD!

Having been greatly encouraged by the reaction of his mother and his praying friend Aunt Violet, particularly, to the news he had shared with them that Sunday afternoon, Chris began to tell anyone who was near enough, or who had time enough, to hear him. Although still very weak, and confined to his bed on his back, he was so thrilled with the sense of peace and joy that had flooded his soul, even in that situation, that he told all the staff, and as many of the patients as came across to speak to him, that he had 'trusted the Lord'. He was saved.

The enthusiasm of this very-ill man for his new 'salvation' was accepted philosophically by some. And cynically by others.

Some listeners, and especially those who knew something of his chequered career to date, expressed a restrained gratification at his exuberant outbursts. Whatever this 'getting saved' was, it could only be better for Chris than where he had come from. So it would probably, 'do him no harm'.

Others, however, were slightly more sceptical. They adopted what had been Linda's initial any-port-in-a-storm-death-bed-conversion type of we-hear-you-but-we-don't-believe-you attitude. Chris would be, they predicted, 'back to normal' in a week of two. They would give him 'a month at the most'.

On Monday morning, though, someone arrived up at the bedside of the by-now-even-stronger and thus-even-happier patient.

It was Beth.

And this Beth, who was a ward auxiliary, was a trifle unusual in that she didn't fit into either of the categories that Chris had encountered in his previous whole-hearted witnessing sessions. She was neither an it-will-probably-help-him or a we-have-heard-hundreds-of-these-headcases-before type.

In all his years of frequent visits to the City Hospital's Ward 2 South, Chris had discovered that there was a super-caring attitude that marked Beth out as someone out of the ordinary. While all the nurses and auxiliaries had always been more than kind to him over his numerous admissions, this auxiliary just had that something extra.

Chris and she had built up an easy rapport, based on years of at-least-once-a-month encounters. They had often exchanged a barrage of good-natured banter.

Beth had always been that bit different, and her reaction to the news she heard when she came on duty that Monday morning, was certainly different.

As she approached his bed Chris knew that she knew that something significant had happened in his life. Her face was beaming, her eyes were sparkling, and when she came close enough for Chris and the whole ward, but not the whole hospital, to hear, she exclaimed, "Oh Chris, I have just heard that you have got saved! That is great news. It is marvellous! Wonderful! Praise the Lord!"

The sick man in the bed smiled back, warmly. He couldn't do anything else. Beth's spiritual faith and fervour were infectious.

Propping herself up in a half-standing half-sitting position at the end of his bed, she went on to explain to Chris why hearing of his salvation had moved her so mightily. And had left her so thrilled.

"You probably never knew it, Chris, but ever since you first came in here, and I don't know how long that is ago now, we have been praying for you every lunch time in our little prayer group. There are three or four of us meet every day for about ten or fifteen minutes in our lunch break. And we have been making you, and your salvation, a matter of special prayer," she informed the confounded new Christian.

Again, Chris was touched to tears as he had been with Aunt Violet's declaration of the previous afternoon.

"Thank you, Beth," he replied with genuine gratitude. "Thank you. I am only now beginning to realize how many people there were praying for me and I knew nothing about it. I find it amazing. Amazing to the extent that it is almost scary. It makes me feel so humble. So useless. So unworthy. And it also makes me feel really privileged to know really good Christian people like you."

Beth bowed her head and blushed a bit. She didn't normally receive such tremendous tidings and such candid compliments all within the space of an hour every Monday morning!

Although Chris felt himself pleased, and also privileged as he had said, he had to confess that there was another small matter about which he found himself just a trifle puzzled.

So he decided to ask Beth about it. Who else? He had sought her assistance with many other matters over the past few years and now that she was sitting there at his bedside in praise-the-Lord!-mode, perhaps she could help him with this one, too.

"Beth, you say that you and your friends have been praying for me every day," he began.

"Yes, that's right," the auxiliary interrupted him, with a reassuring grin. "We have."

"Well, why is it that you have been praying for ME particularly, or specifically, or what ever you said it was? Do you not pray for all these other guys around here?" he enquired, waving a loose arm through a one-hundred-and-eighty-degree sweep around the ward.

"Yes, we do pray for all the patients on the ward," Beth replied, having lowered her voice to an almost-whisper, just in case some of 'these other guys' would take offence at her response. Not that she thought that they could care enough to be bothered, but she considered it best to be careful.

"We made your illness and your salvation a matter of special prayer, for two particular reasons, Chris," she continued, in an attempt to answer his question. "The first of these was a purely personal one. You have been in here so often, that we know you so well. You are like an old familiar friend or even a brother, to some of us."

The caring Christian auxiliary paused before proceeding, and in her pause she turned her head towards the bedside locker. As she did so, Chris noticed that she focused her gaze on something sitting there.

"That little red Gideon New Testament is the second reason why we have all been praying so long and so earnestly for you," she admitted with a quaint smile. "All the Christian staff have noticed that every time you come in here for treatment you have that little New Testament with you. We thought when we saw it, and the unashamed way in which you always displayed it on your locker, that you must have had some interest in the things of God, and that perhaps God was dealing with you somehow. So we have just been praying that you would read your Testament, and come to Jesus."

When she had completed her very understandable explanation about the Gideon New Testament, Chris told her the story of his attachment to it. He recalled for her those wild, rough, tough, skinhead, drunken, drug-drop-out days when it had been his constant companion, his 'lucky charm', and the unlikely in-bag partner for a two foot long machete with a razor-sharp blade!

It was then Beth's turn to be astonished, but she could understand this strange attraction to the little red book, to some extent. Nor was she afraid to give the credit to Whom she was sure the credit was due.

"Praise the Lord!" she called out, as loudly as she thought she dare. "And praise the Lord again!"

This spontaneous outburst from Beth expressed precisely how many folks felt.

Chris, his mother, Aunt Violet and her 'wee fellowship', and Beth and her lunch time prayer group, all believed that they had a lot for which they ought to 'praise the Lord'.

And they did it too!

For weeks!

18

COLD TURKEY

Chris was saved. Praise the Lord! His fear of death had gone, but the prospect of continued life, even as a Christian, still presented him with a few problems.

Although he now had a deep sense of spiritual peace in his soul, he still had physical and mental torment in his embattled body.

Since he had been on intravenous morphine for three weeks for the relief of real or 'imagined' pain, and with his previous history of drug-dependence, Chris was now addicted to the legally prescribed drug. He was 'high as a kite'. All the time.

So, when they were satisfied that their patient was making satisfactory progress after his operation, and was no longer in urgent need of pain-relieving drugs, the hospital doctors made their decision. And that decision was set to trigger another crisis in the colourful life of Chris.

"We are not going to give you any more medication, Chris," they informed the new convert in the old body. "There will be no more morphine for you. In fact there will be no more medicine of any sort. Not even so much as a headache tablet. We are going to have to 'cold turkey' you."

Although he dreaded the thought of it, Chris knew that the 'cold turkey' experience was the only way out of his addiction. For in addition to improving both his mental and physical condition, it would also help to strengthen him spiritually. It would provide reinforcements for Soul in the Body versus Soul battle that had begun to rage in his mind soon after he had simply accepted Christ as his Saviour that night before his operation. It should help him to crawl away from, like a snake splitting its skin and then slithering away, the casual and careless attitudes of his former lifestyle.

But it would be hard. Tough. All uphill.

Chris knew that as a Christian the lying had to stop. There could be no more play-acted pretences of unbearable pain to obtain another series of shots of morphine. Yet his addicted body was screaming out for the drug ceaselessly, constantly, continuously. Day and night.

What was Chris to do? It was a battle. And perhaps even more than a battle. It seemed more like all-out war, sometimes.

And 'cold turkey' could provide the answer.

No drugs. But the final blow.

No morphine. But the winning manoeuvre.

No pain-killers. But the path to peace.

No question. Had to be done. But no fun.

A week after his operation, all treatment of Chris ceased. His sustaining stream of drugs dried up

No pills. No injections. No apologies. No mercy.

Nothing.

And since morphine as a drug is both physically and psychologically addictive, the withdrawal symptoms upon the ceasing of all dosage of it, are both physically and psychologically experienced. In excruciating fashion.

Soon after he was left without his stimulating 'fixes' Chris was glad that he was now a Christian. For he began to pray for the strength and determination to go through the 'cold turkey' experience, and come out safely on the other side.

It was desperately difficult, though.

He began to break out in hot and cold sweats alternately. His muscles seized up and became very painful. Goose pimples formed all over his fiercely itching skin. A body covered with these unsightly swellings very much resembles the skin of a big plucked turkey, hence the name 'cold turkey'. An apt nickname for an agonizing ordeal.

Occasionally his heart would beat frantically as though attempting to hammer its way out of his chest. These palpitations prompted Chris to summon the nursing staff, time and time again, with the despairing cry, "Get me something quickly nurse. I am having a heart attack!"

All such frantic pleas were invariably met with a barely discernible hint of a smile and a very definite shake of the head.

It was awful.

And if the physical agony of 'cold turkey' was bad, the mental torment was perhaps even worse.

Chris was constantly overwhelmed with the weird sensation of being a prisoner in his own mind. He had horrific nightmares. Uninvited images from his earlier chequered career cascaded around in complete confusion. And he never seemed to be able to rid himself of them, however hard he tried.

For days and nights Chris couldn't sleep. He was so agitated.

At night, when all the other patients had attempted to settle for the night the churning Chris couldn't even settle for any more than ten minutes at any one time. Then either the anguish of his body or the misery in his mind, had him jumping up and leaning on the buzzer.

If it wasn't a 'heart attack' he was having, it was either the pains in his legs or his arms.

Or perhaps he had even dared to close his eyes and frightening figures had besieged his brain. These horrendous hallucinations terrified Chris, sending him into an absolute blind panic.

The only solace that he could find was in prayer. In talking to God. He had often tried to read his little red Testament but he couldn't concentrate long enough to gain any comfort from it at that time.

But praying was different. He could do it at any time. And did. These prayers, which were spawned in discomfort and distraction, were not long and complicated, but terse and to the point.

"Lord, help me! Please help me! Please help me through this. Here. Now. This minute!" was about standard length for a 'cold turkey' panic prayer.

While living through this experience was very trying for Chris, it also proved to be an extreme test of the patience of an extremely patient staff.

After a few days and nights of continual interruption the staff made another decision which was also to prove a test of the physical, mental, and now also spiritual, strength, of Chris the 'cold-turkeyed' Christian.

"You can go home today, Chris," the consultant informed him one afternoon. "As your operation appears to have been successful, and since we are not planning to give you any further medication at present, you can go home later on today."

Home. Home!

Did I hear the man right? Chris wondered, the cold sweat streaming down his face. How will I ever manage to get home?

And how will I ever survive if I ever get there?

19

'THE DARKNESS DEEPENS'

It was seven o'clock in the evening when Linda arrived up to the City Hospital in Belfast to take her husband home. She had arranged for her mother to keep Samantha so that she would have time to see Chris settled in, and find out if he could possibly cope at home, before bringing their little daughter back to join them.

When he had said his 'good-byes' to the somewhat sad, but not altogether heartbroken, staff on the ward, Chris, helped by Linda, for he could barely walk more than twenty yards unaided, made it out to the car in the hospital car park.

As they were driving between Belfast and Lisburn, on their way home to the Old Warren, Chris, though still physically very weak, turned to his wife , and said, much to her surprise, "Linda, there is somewhere I want you to take me before we go home."

This, thought Linda, is the test. Where does he want to go?

Usually, when Chris had been either too debilitated, too drunk, or too drugged, to drive himself, he had asked her to drive him to either one of three places. It would either be the pub, the bookies, or the off-licence.

Which will it be this evening? she wondered.

I will see now how real his conversion is, she concluded.

"Are you sure you are well enough to go anywhere other than your bed, Chris?" she asked initially, with genuine good-wife concern.

"I'm not feeling great to tell you the truth," Chris replied, honestly, "but there is somewhere I really need to go, before I do anything else."

"And where is that?" Linda enquired further, her curiosity aroused by the earnest nature of her still-ill husband's expressed desire. This intense insistence appeared to her unusual, for Chris was normally an easy-going sort of character who never really became 'fired-up' about things unless he was either in a fight or full-drunk. And today he was neither.

"I want to go to church. To the church where we were married. I want you to take me round to St. Columba's. I hope it's open," came the totally unexpected reply. "O.K. we can go there, no problem," Linda complied, both mildly amused and greatly amazed. She was happy to be baffled by this one.

As far as she could recall, she could never ever remember Chris going to church. To the best of her knowledge he had seldom, if ever, been inside a place of worship, since they were married in St. Columba's Presbyterian Church almost four years before. And now, since it was obviously the only one that he felt that he had, in any sense, some sort of a connection to, he wanted to go back there!

So it wasn't the pub he wanted to go to for his first stop out of hospital!

And it wasn't the bookies!

Nor was it even the off-licence for a stock-up!

It was a church!

When they arrived at St. Columba's and approached the door, Chris wondered if they would get in. It all seemed so closed up. So quiet. So sacred, somehow.

It would be a disappointment to him if he couldn't fulfil this first desire. He so much longed to be in 'God's house'. When he had been told that he could 'go home', Chris had determined to begin life outside the confines of the hospital in the sanctity of a church, if at all possible.

Linda pushed the door. And it opened.

Great! They were in!

Then they walked almost on tip-toe, feeling a funny sense of being like legitimate trespassers, through the porch, and into the main body of the church.

Chris sank, exhausted, into the aisle-edge of a pew, three rows from the back.

He was physically drained and mentally fuzzy, but nonetheless he was still spiritually exuberant.

Linda stood nervously in the aisle watching in wonder, and listening in absolute awe, as her husband who had once been so defiant, and so disinterested in all things Christian, bowed his head and in few simple sentences thanked God for saving him. He also asked Him for the strength to face what lay ahead in the days and months to come. The returning prodigal prayed for the love and wisdom to be a good husband and father, from that day on, and for the courage to tell all his 'mates' about his salvation. He wasn't really looking forward to that, but knew it had to be done.

Unseen by the head-almost-down-between-his knees passionately praying Chris, Linda hastily wiped away a tear from the corner of her eye.

After a few moments of silent meditation, Chris raised his head.

"Thanks, Linda. That's O.K. We can go on now," he said, struggling unsteadily to his feet. The sweat was pouring down his face again.

But his serene smile summed up the whole situation.

Despite the utter weakness of his drug-craving body and the recurring panic of his drug-crazed mind, he was happy, deep down.

And it showed, it shone out, below, and through, it all.

As they made their way tortuously back to the car, Chris had another idea. There was another visit he felt he should make.

On the way up from Belfast he had remembered that it was Wednesday night. And Wednesday night was band practice night.

Having fulfilled his first ambition, to call in the church, Chris now felt that he ought to call into the band hall too, and see them all. He had been a drummer in Broomhedge Pipe Band for many years, and many of the band members had been very kind to him during his stay in hospital.

He was sure that most of them would know by now that he had 'turned good livin'' as they called it, for some of them had been interested enough to even come and visit him in 'The City' and he had told them then of his salvation. Nonetheless it would be good to pay them a courtesy call, he felt.

"Could you take me over to the band hall, Linda?" he decided to broach the subject, just as the patient driver was starting the engine. He wondered what his wife's response would be. She had been good enough to take him to the church. Would she consider him fit enough to take in the band hall as well?

Linda, for her part, though realizing how totally drained he was, also knew how much his stop over at the church had meant to him.

No doubt there would turn out to be some good reason for a 'drop in' on practice night, too.

"I can easily if you are up to it," she replied, again with a caution conceived in tender loving care.

"Yes, I think I can make it," Chris told her, and then backed up his assertion with a single assurance. "I promise you that if you take me to the band-hall there will be no more requests after that. I will probably be glad to go straight home I can tell you!"

So Linda drove to the hall where the band members had gathered for their weekly practice.

It was after eight o'clock when Chris arrived in the drumming room, followed by his wife, a discreet two or three steps behind. She again wondered what all this was all about.

As the slowly shuffling figure of Chris entered the drumming room, all drumming stopped.

Some of his former-fellow-drummers called out, "Great to see you, Chris! How are you?"

Others just stared, unsure of what do say.

They had heard the Chris had 'seen the light', were pleased to see him well enough to be out of hospital, but were shocked at the shaky, sickly state of their once strong friend. Now they doubted, for a number of reasons, if he would ever be back.

Hence, not knowing what to say to be sensible, they said nothing.

Chris greeted them all with a "Nice to see you all again," but barely stopped in his tracks. He was on his way into the main hall where the bagpipe players were tuning up.

Linda followed, fascinated.

When he entered the 'pipe' room, again the cacophony of sound ceased.

And again most of the pipers welcomed their one-time-drumming partner.

"Great to see you, Chris," some of them shouted, repeating the sentiments of the drummers, two minutes before.

"You are looking well," somebody else added. That, Chris felt. was stretching it a bit. For if he was looking well, he certainly didn't **feel** well.

His reserve of strength had almost gone.

His legs had begun to shake uncontrollably.

"I can't stay long," he said, flopping, rather than sitting, down on a convenient chair. "But there is something I would like some of you to do for me."

Then, without even waiting for any reaction from his silent-bagpipe-bearing audience, he continued, "Could some of you play 'Abide With Me', for me?"

"Certainly. Gladly, no problem," one of the girls responded with a smile, and before any of the others could even get their chanter to their lips, she had begun.

Others, who had been going to play folded their pipes back under their arms.

Slowly, stealthily, and almost eerily, the haunting air of 'Abide With Me', played perfectly, filled the room.

Chris had heard that tune played often. And in hospital he had often hummed it to himself, in some of his bleakest hours.

Sitting there, transfixed, in that band hall that evening, however, he thought of the words of some of the verses. Words that he had heard audiences sing on many occasions.

'Abide with me ; fast falls the eventide ;
The darkness deepens ; Lord, with me abide ;
When other helpers fail, and comforts flee,
Help of the helpless, oh, abide with me!...

I fear no foe with Thee at hand to bless,
Ills have no weight, and tears no bitterness ;
Where is death's sting ? where, grave thy victory ?
I triumph still if Thou abide with me.'

'The darkness deepens'. How he had experienced that in the past week or so.   He had been saved, and he was glad about that.

The fear of death had gone. The sting had been extracted. He was glad about that, too.

But the struggle through 'cold turkey' had been tough.

It had seemed as though it would eventually overpower him. Close him down, or snuff him out.

Through it all there had been one ray of light and hope that had kept him going. It was the fact that although the darkness had indeed deepened, the Lord had always been 'abiding' with him.

And then there was that last verse.

What a comfort it was. And how the truth of it had even been proved that very evening.

'I fear no foe, with Thee at hand to bless....'

There he was. Sitting in a band hall with a number of men and women, many of whom had no time for God, or indeed anything even remotely 'religious'.

Yet they had all welcomed him warmly.

Had even lied that he was 'looking well'!

The Lord who had saved him had proved that he could keep him. And would 'abide with' him. In any and every circumstance of life.

The strains of the pipes had died away.

An almost reverent silence settled for a second or two over the band hall.

And an everlasting sense of peace had settled over Chris's soul.

He was now ready for home.

20

GALLONS OF DRINK, ALL DOWN THE SINK!

It was a totally worn-out-and-ready-to-drop Chris Killen who arrived back with his wife Linda to their home in Old Warren, Lisburn, later that evening.

Any little reserve of energy he had built up in hospital had long since been sapped away. But his soul was satisfied.

The gradually-clearing cloud of confusion, and the less frequent, but still present, periods of blind panic, occasionally threatened to master his mind again. But he was happy in the Lord.

Chris had spoken to God in grateful prayer, in church, and he had seen his friends in the Broomhedge Pipe Band, who appeared to respect his position as a Christian. The solo rendition of 'Abide With Me' had been wonderful, too. Such an inspiration and consolation.

On the last lap homeward Chris had been anticipating how marvellous it would be to just tumble into bed, at last. It would he great, just to rest his battled body, and close his aching eyes...

When he reached the house, however, he found that it didn't quite work out that way. He discovered that he wasn't altogether ready to forget everything else and roll into bed. Not yet. For a while at least.

Newly arrived home after more than three weeks away, Chris found that he just wanted to walk around, and sit about, and savour the security of the familiarity of his home environment. He began to lift everyday things and examine them closely. He gazed intently at photographs that had been there for years. And a few of the more recent ones of baby Samantha.

The astounding thing was that he seemed to be seeing everything in a new and different light. It was a strange, almost startling, sensation.

On reaching the kitchen in his lingering tour-of-the-downstairs, Chris stopped suddenly in the doorway, as though pulled up short by an invisible but nonetheless powerful set of reins, and focused fixedly on the fridge. The memory of what he had last seen in there jarred him to the bottom of his now-saved soul.

He took three or four steps across the kitchen with as much haste as the spent state of his body would allow. Then he opened the door of the fridge.

What a sight met his gaze!

The fridge was full, jam-packed full, of alcoholic drink of all kinds!

There were cans and bottles of beer and lager. They seemed to be fighting for a place in the tray on the door and in six-packs on the shelves. One shelf had been removed to allow the bigger bottles of wine, gin and vodka to stand up straight and tall at the back.

Small bottles of schnapps, like rows of little toy soldiers, lined the front of the shelves and other single bottles filled in all the remaining available spaces.

There had never ever been much room for food in the Killen fridge. Just drink.

Part of the reason for that could have been that up until that point, they hadn't paid much attention to the need for food in their lives. Just drink. It was the important thing. Along with the drugs.

Drink and drugs had been a part of Chris and Linda's staple diet for months. Perhaps even years.

Chris stood stock still. Rooted to the spot. Spellbound.

Where once the sight of so much booze all in one place would have excited him, he now found that it sickened him.

He didn't want it. Had no desire for it. Felt he must dispose of it. And at once!

"Before I do anything else, Linda, the first thing I must do is get rid of all this drink!" he shouted to his wife, not realizing that she was standing in the doorway he had just left, three yards behind him. Linda had been upstairs packing away some bits and pieces and preparing his bed, and had come down to see what he was doing. And to find out when he was actually intending to go to bed!

"All right, Chris," she replied, the proximity of her presence giving her husband a start. "If that is what you want to do, go ahead!"

She then stood back and watched in total amazement as Chris emptied their fridge.

Can after can was ring-pulled open and their contents poured, foaming and frothing, down the sink.

Bottle after bottle was uncorked or unscrewed, and their contents followed, foaming and frothing, down the sink.

When, after about ten minutes, Chris had finished his banish-the-booze offensive he was left with three distinct and different things. He had a bench littered with empty bottles and cans, a kitchen that smelt worse than any pub he had ever been to in his life, and a deep settled peace in his soul.

The enduring consolation of the third of these more than compensated for temporary inconvenience of the other two.

Having watched the last of his stockpile of drink drain away, Chris turned to Linda and said, wearily, "I think I will go to bed, now."

His wife was glad to hear that. She was sure he should have been in bed two hours ago!

"O.K. Chris," she replied. "You go on upstairs. I will clear up here for you."

When she was satisfied that he could make his own way up to the bedroom, Linda returned to the kitchen and surveyed the scene.

It was now her turn to stand stock still.

As she looked over at the cans and bottles, piled in a higgledy-piggledy dribbling heap on the workbench, she was overcome by that same sense of absolute awe that she had felt when Chris had poured out his heart in thankfulness to God in the church.

Something miraculous had definitely happened in her husband's life.

Firstly there had been the stopping of the swearing. Then telling Aunt Violet about his conversion. Earlier this evening she had witnessed the praying in the church. And the request for 'Abide With Me' in the band hall.

But this, now, was the most incredible thing of all. Gallons of drink, all down the sink.

There could be no doubt about it, the Chris who had come out of hospital was an entirely different person to the Chris who had gone in.

In spite of his illness he now seemed to have a totally new life about him.

There seemed to be a new spirit within him, somehow.

And secretly she longed to have it too.

21

SELL THEM OFF, OR SMASH THEM UP?

News, whether considered good or bad, travels fast.

So it was with the conversion of Chris. The chief talking-point in the drink and drugs sub-culture in Lisburn, over the next few days, became the fact that Chris Killen had 'turned good-living'. The word soon spread around, 'He says he's 'saved', if you know what that means.'

Some of his former associates knew Chris well. And they also knew quite well that if it was true, and Chris **had** become a Christian, then they were hardly ever likely to see him with them, around his old haunts, again. He certainly wouldn't want to be seen 'hanging out', as they described their casual spending-time-and-money loose association, with them any more. They would probably soon discover that he had started to go to church a lot, and read and talk about the Bible.

All the gossip about Chris having 'turned religious', and having 'given up the booze and come off the drugs', gave one of his friends a bright idea.

This man knew for a fact that Chris had a massive collection of hard-rock records which he had built up over many years. If Chris was now 'converted' he wouldn't need them any more. Well, would he? If he was going to start to go to church, in line with some of the other lads' very confident prediction, he would be starting to sing hymns and psalms and things like that. Nor would he have any time, or use, for his hard-rock records.

So, one night, he arrived up at the door of the Killen home in Old Warren.

"I say, Chris," he began, when Linda had called her husband to the door, "I believe you have been 'saved' and have given up your old life. I suppose us fellas will hardly see much more of you."

"That's right," Chris replied, "I was saved there that last time I was in the hospital. And yes. You are right about the other thing as well. You probably won't be seeing a lot of me from now on."

Not wanting to be cornered by a 'religious freak', and yet extremely anxious to get his hands on what he knew his friend had somewhere in that house, the man at the door went on hurriedly, "I was just wondering, Chris, if you would sell me some of your records. You must have hundreds of them that you won't be needing any more. I will give you a good price for some of them!"

That, to Chris, sounded like a fair deal.

He definitely would never need them any more. Those records would never, ever be played again in his house. And this man wanted what he didn't need. And was willing to pay him for them.

So Chris invited him in, and for almost an hour that hard-rock fan sifted through his vast stock of offensive music. And made his selection.

Then he did what he promised he would do. He gave Chris 'a good price for them'.

The customer left the house happy, for he reckoned that he had made a great deal. Even at 'a good price'.

The seller, however, was not quite so happy.

True, he had the money, the 'good price', in his pocket.

But his conscience pricked him.

'This is not right', he concluded, as he returned to the living-room where records in assorted sizes, and sleeves in garish colours, were strewn on the chairs, on the settee, on top of the TV, and all across the floor.

'I am peddling the devil's music,' he thought. 'And that just can not be right. That stuff I have just sold to that mate is downright evil. Blatantly bad. It is unashamedly racist. And anti-God, anti-establishment, anti-everything normally acceptable.'

He stood for a few moments contemplating his next move. And he knew what would soon be happening. It wouldn't be long until there would be a steady stream of prospective buyers at his door offering to relieve him of all stock now 'surplus to requirements'. All 'for a good price', of course.

It was time to act. And to act decisively.

Chris strode out to the shed in the back yard and found his hammer. Then he returned resolutely to the living-room.

One by one he picked up the records and read the labels.

Skrewdriver...The Cockney Rejects...Anti-Nowhere League...

And one by one he set them on the floor and smashed them to pieces with the hammer.

When he came to one particular record he hesitated, held it up, and then turned it over slowly. A quaint smile began to play at the corners of his mouth as he recalled the price he had paid for it. His boots!

That record, by a group called Combat 18 was so offensive that it had been banned in Britain. Chris, however, had seen a German guy with it in London and he had bartered the boots he was wearing for it! He had so badly wanted the record, and the German skinhead had so badly wanted, perhaps even needed, a new pair of boots, that they had agreed a simple swop.

Chris had walked back to his hotel in his sock soles, clutching his prize acquisition, such a 'rare' record, and the German had gone home, all pleased too, in a pair of long leather boots!

It had to go as well, though.

There could be no room for sentiment here.

The message of utter hatred which that specific record sought to convey, couched in language so foul that Chris could no longer bear the thought of even hearing, not to mention using, had no place in a Christian's home.

It had to be totally decommissioned.

Nobody should ever hear it again.

So it was duly placed in the middle of the floor amid the splinters of all the other already-dealt-with offenders. Then, bang! It too, came under the hammer. Literally.

Nobody **would** ever hear it again!

When Linda came in to see what was going on, Chris had just finished. She found him sitting in the middle of the floor, surrounded on all sides by mutilated records. Some had been smashed into smithereens. Others had ended up in crazy crumpled shapes, held together by their labels.

It was a mess.

But there again, despite the chaos, which could, no doubt, like the kitchen of a few nights before, be cleared, Chris was serenely happy. He was at peace with himself, and had a clear conscience towards God.

Another hurdle had been overcome, and another bridge back to his former life had been burnt.

On the next evening, when two more of Chris's former accomplices came around to their door, offering to buy some records, at 'a fair price', Linda informed them that the 'Great Clearance Sale' had come to an abrupt end. And then she told them a smashing story.

That strange news, too, soon spread amongst the hard man, hard rock, hard drugs, fraternity in Lisburn.

'You needn't bother going back up to Killen's,' was the message on the grape-vine.

'There are no more records for sale up there.

At a good price. At a fair price. Or, indeed, at any price.

Chris has smashed them all!'

22

WHAT BRINGS YOU HERE?

The exceptional change in the life of Chris Killen made a tremendous impact upon his wife. Linda was always expecting Chris to slip up with a swear word, slip off to the off-licence, or slip away for a 'fix', but it didn't happen.

She now had, for the first time since they were married, a considerate stay-at-home husband, and Samantha had a caring father, for the first time in her short life. Both of them were, too, probably without recognizing it at the time, living under the same roof as someone who had started to pray fervently for them, dozens of times per day. Soon after his own conversion Chris became increasingly burdened by the intolerable realization that although he was now saved, and on his way to heaven, Linda, his partner in life, was still lost, and on her way to hell. This frightened him and spurred him into incessant and impassioned prayer.

Not only did Chris pray for his wife, however, but he also spoke to her about salvation, shared verses he had discovered in the Bible with her, and invited her to join him at the meetings he attended in Lisburn Pentecostal Fellowship.

Linda had no objection to going with Chris to the meetings. It certainly proved much simpler to accompany him home from a meeting, sober and attentive, than to escort him home from a pub, full-drunk and abusive.

When she began to attend these meetings at first Linda had a problem with the concept of salvation by grace. What she could never seem to understand was why God would ever be interested in her. Indeed He was so concerned about her that He sent His Son to die for her on Calvary, was what the preachers claimed! Surely the God who had created the universe, and kept it all perfectly in place, would have more to worry about than one insignificant wife and mother, living in a small housing-estate, in a big town, in a small province, in a big world!

She knew that she needed to be saved, though, and gradually she realized that she wanted to be saved. If being a Christian had brought such controlling peace and lasting satisfaction into Chris's life, it could probably do the same for her.

On Saturday, 14th October 1989, Linda set out, with Chris, to a special rally in his church. The service that evening had been billed as 'a testimony meeting when a group of lads from The Shore Road in Belfast will tell what God has done in their lives.'

It could prove interesting.

As they approached the hall where the meeting was to be held, Linda had made up her mind. This was the night. She was going to speak to 'Aunt' Violet about becoming a Christian, after the meeting. That was definite. There could be no more 'messing about' on this matter.

On the way into the church, where the congregation was beginning to gather, Linda spotted Violet up ahead. Quickening her pace she caught up with the older, slower lady and placing a hand on her shoulder said simply, "Aunt Violet, I want a wee word with you afterwards."

"O.K. Linda," came the reply, "I will wait out here for you."

This lady of prayer had no idea what was on Linda's mind so she gave it no further thought. It was probably to arrange for her to call round to see Samantha, who by that time was growing fast, and doing or saying something new or interesting every day, it seemed.

When Chris and Linda entered the church, Chris was thrilled to see 'Davy' sitting two rows in front of them. This Davy had been a member of the same gang as him in his bathful-of-beer Mount Vernon days. They had often drunk themselves senseless, or shot up on dope, together.

'That's great to see Davy in a meeting' was the instant inward reaction of Chris to discovering his former accomplice 'under the sound of the Gospel'.

Wouldn't it be marvellous if Davy could just get saved!

Leaning forward in his seat, Chris gave an exaggerated whisper across the empty row between them, "Davy!"

Davy turned around sharply and saw Chris behind him. The look of wonder on his face was matched only by the new convert's wonder and sense of disbelief at him being there!

Rising at once from his seat Davy came back down to where Chris and Linda were sitting.

"Good to see you again Davy," Chris greeted him. "And what brings you here?
Have you come up with these guys from the Shore Road?"

"Yes, I have, Chris," Davy replied, happiness etched all over him. "I have come to give my testimony. I came to know the Lord just last year. But let me ask you the same question. What brings **you** here?"

To the obvious delight, and perhaps the mild amusement of some of the more 'senior' members of the assembling congregation, there followed scenes of unrestrained delight as Chris and Davy shook each other's hands enthusiastically and slapped each other vigorously on the back.

While the two erstwhile skinheads were rejoicing together, totally oblivious to her, Linda was sitting reflecting on the question they had both been so interested to have answered.

'And what brings you here?'

Linda became even more resolute. She knew, even if they didn't, what had brought **her** there. She wanted to be saved, and as satisfied, as they were.

After a few more 'Praise the Lord!'s and one almighty final 'Hallelujah!' Davy resumed his seat beside the others, and the meeting began.

There was an atmosphere of down-to-earth sincerity about the entire service. These guys who had come to speak had dramatic stories to tell of what God had done for them, and they were prepared to recount those stories in their own language. What they had to say was not clouded by complicated theology or meaningless, hackneyed phrases. It was all straight-from-the-shoulder straight-from-the-heart stuff. The spellbound audience knew they were getting the truth, the whole truth, and nothing but the truth.

And the night of sanctified surprises wasn't over yet either!

When another of the 'group from the Shore Road' who had come 'to testify' stood up, Chris recognized him at once!

This chap had been one of his former 'enemies'. He was a Roman Catholic, from the other side of 'the Peace Line'. Chris and he had often traded insults, and punches, with each other.

Now he was a Christian!

When this young man had almost finished the compelling account of his conversion he paused briefly before proceeding, almost, it seemed, with a sense of compulsion shaded by reluctance.

"I have never done this before," he continued hesitantly, " but somehow I feel led to say this. There is somebody in this meeting who really wants to be saved. And I want you to know that the Lord really wants to save you too! Now. Right here. Tonight."

Those words struck like flaming arrows into Linda's heart. The time had come for action.

At the close of the service the church pastor, George Sands, invited anyone who wanted to 'give their lives to the Lord' to join him 'in the room at the back.'

And Linda did just that.

As others were filing out at the front, murmuring about 'the great meeting', she said under her breath to her overjoyed husband, "I want to go in there,' and the pair of them made their way towards the specified 'room at the back'.

Unknown to them someone else had seen them as they had slipped, as they thought, unobtrusively, forward. Just as they were greeting Pastor Sands, and were about to close the door it was pushed open again.

Aunt Violet had prayed for more than twenty years for this moment. So there was no way that she was going to miss it now, if at all possible!

Linda was broken.

She sat with Chris on one side and 'Aunt' Violet on the other. Pastor Sands and Clarke, the leader of 'the group from the Shore Road', sat across from them.

It was quite obvious to everyone that God was at work in Linda's life, but Pastor Sands wanted to be sure. It would be best to hear it from her own mouth.

"What's the matter, Linda?" he enquired, gently.

"I would like to be saved. I have done for some time now, but tonight really spoke to me," came the half-whispered reply.

George Sands nodded. He understood.

Opening his Bible he then began to read a verse from Matthew chapter eleven. It said, 'Come unto me, all ye that labour and are heavy laden, and I will give you rest'

When he had read some other verses that Linda had heard quoted often before in the meetings, since she had started to come with Chris, the pastor went on to explain that God had invited her, and was waiting for her to come. Regardless of how unworthy or insignificant she felt God had promised to receive her, and give her rest from her burden of sin.

In a few moment's time he closed his Bible softly and told Linda that he was going to pray with her, and for her, and suggested that as he prayed audibly she could also pray silently, inviting Jesus to come into her life, and be her Saviour.

Linda had come to that point where she was happy to do as Pastor Sands had suggested, and so as he was finishing his prayer Linda had just begun to make her own silent supplication. She simply confessed her sin and accepted Christ as Lord and Saviour.

An amazing time of rejoicing followed.

Husband and wife were now united, not only by the bonds of matrimony, but also in faith in Christ. Aunt Violet sat in shining silence, shining tears streaming down her shining face. She had seen another of her prayers answered. It was fantastic.

Later that evening when Chris and Linda arrived home, both happy in the Lord, Linda could barely wait to tell her mother, who had been keeping Samantha, the news.

As soon as she entered the living-room and saw that her mother was rising to meet her, Linda burst out spontaneously, almost involuntarily, "Oh mummy, I have got saved!"

Louise Castles stepped across and hugged her daughter.

"That is wonderful, Linda! Really wonderful!" she responded, just as spontaneously, and certainly just as sincerely, as had been her daughter's exclamation.

Then she began to weep, too.

She knew exactly what 'being saved' meant, for she had been brought up in a Christian home, and her Aunt Violet had lived with her family for years, also.

Linda's mum knew exactly what 'being saved' meant. In others.

She herself was not a Christian, though. Not yet.

But the band of people praying for her had been increased again by another one.

First there had been her parents. And Aunt Violet.

Then came her son-in-law, Chris.

And now there was her just-saved daughter, Linda.

23

CASTLES UNITED

In just the same way that the change in Chris's life had affected his wife, so the dramatic change in the life and attitude of her daughter and the transformation in the Killen home made an inescapable impression on Linda's mother.

Although Louise Castles had known about salvation, and had seen it lived out in her home from childhood, this about-turn for the better in the lifestyle of her daughter and son-in-law had the most profound impact upon her of anything to date.

It was amazing in their home now.

Instead of consuming endless cans and bottles of drink, and shouting and swearing at each other, Chris and Linda were now reading the Bible together. And the tape player, which had once blasted out hard rock from morning until night was now being used to play comforting Christian hymns!

There could be no mistaking the fact that God had entered their home. To stay. He had become, in the words of a plaque she remembered seeing somewhere, on somebody's wall, in her earlier, travelling-around-Christian-homes-with-Christian- parents days, 'the unseen Guest at every meal, and the silent Listener to every conversation.'

Shortly after her own conversion Linda had asked her mother if she would like 'to come along' to church with Chris and her every Sunday evening.

Mum was not hard to persuade. Louise Castles accepted her daughter's invitation quite happily. And Aunt Violet began to pray all the more fervently.

For months Chris and Linda collected the interested and influenced mother and brought her along to the Sunday evening services in their church.

And for months they joined the faithful Aunt Violet in prayer for her conversion.

In May, 1990, a special Gospel mission was being conducted in another church in Lisburn, and Chris and Linda brought Linda's mum along, on as many nights as she was free to attend. They knew that God had begun to work in her life. She was seeking salvation. Although not admitting it openly the obvious peace that Chris and Linda had found was what she craved.

On Thursday 24th May all three of them were at the meeting, and on that night Sid Murray and his wife Lily, from Belfast, had been invited to recount their amazing story of conversion.

It was Lily's story which particularly gripped Louise Castles. As this woman told of a life of empty recklessness, and of how, when about to throw herself off a bridge in a fit of blind depression, she had been arrested and stopped by some Invisible Power, and then later saved, Louise Castles realized that the God who had realigned the life of Lily Murray could do the same for her. She determined that she would not let another night pass. Tonight would be the night when she too would be saved.

When the invitation was extended, at the close of the service, for 'anybody who wanted to speak to the pastor about salvation' to come forward, Chris and Linda were delighted, if somewhat taken aback momentarily, when Linda's mother rose from where she had been sitting beside her daughter, and made her way forward for counselling.

Linda followed her, a few paces behind, and in a room at the back the church pastor read some verses from the Bible and prayed with the anxious mother, and she came to know Christ as Saviour.

More wonderful news! Another one for Aunt Violet to transfer across from the 'Pray for salvation' to the 'Pray for strength and sustenance' sections of her lengthy prayer list.

Now they began to pray for Linda's father. William Castles was still not a Christian, and although he had actually encouraged his wife to attend every available church service with their daughter and son-in-law he had not been so keen to go along himself. Fair enough, he had marvelled at the miraculous transformation in his daughter Linda's home circumstances, but all this religious stuff, and going out to Church and meetings, nearly every night of the week, as it seemed to him, was not for him.

What he had totally underestimated, though, was the power of prayer. Violet's praying army had been increased by one, again. Now Chris, Linda and his wife Louise had all joined her, in praying for him.

For more than a year they prayed. And talked to William.

The biggest influence in his life, though, then began to be his wife. Now that Louise was saved she had begun to read the Bible every day, and to listen to Christian music at all times of the day and night. One of her favourites was the singing of Rev. William McCrea.

As those tapes were played, and turned over, played and turned over, day after day, her husband never objected. The truth was that, although it would not be in keeping with his 'neutral' stance to admit it, he rather enjoyed the music. And what was more interesting, though again, one could not admit it, was that the message of the music had started to get through to him.

Then, in the summer of 1991, he began to respond, rather half-heartedly at first, to the repeated invitations to join the others in attending church services. He would go with them occasionally. Just to keep them happy. They all seemed so happy, so it would be best to keep them that way!

On Monday 14th October, 1991, Rev. William Mc Crea had been invited to sing and speak at the Harvest Service in Lisburn Free Presbyterian Church, which by that time Chris and Linda had begun to attend. William Castles agreed readily to go with the family to that special service. William Mc Crea had sung to him so often out of a black tape-recorder on the sideboard it would be something different to hear the man 'live', he reckoned.

Through what he had heard, and what he had witnessed in the lives of those he loved, William had often considered salvation over the past number of months in a casual, off-hand manner. He promised himself that he would 'attend to that sometime', just in the same way as he was going to 'sort out' the weeds in the flower bed at the front or the rattle in the boot of the car.

He could not have anticipated, though, what was set to happen to him in that service.

As William Mc Crea sang a piece called, 'How Many Tears Shall Dim Your Eye?' Linda's dad was touched. It was the chorus, particularly, which challenged him, every time it came around.

The words seemed to echo into his soul...

'Come as you are, God's grace is free,
The Lord is good, come taste and see,
Now is the time, what will you do,
Can't you hear God's voice, He is calling you?'

When he had finished singing Rev. Mc Crea commenced to speak, referring in the course of his address to a verse from the Bible. It was Second Corinthians chapter five, and verse seventeen. 'Therefore if any man be in Christ, he is a new creature: old things are passed away; behold, all things are become new.'

As the preacher continued speaking, contrasting the old and the new man, the old and the new nature, and the change which being 'in Christ' could make, William Castles had to admit that it was true. He had seen it in practice. And at first-hand. In his home. And in his family. The evidence was all lined up beside him. Chris, Linda, Louise.

That night he too recognized that he needed the change of heart and of life, which only Christ could give. More importantly, however, he also realized that he actually **wanted** the change of heart and of life which only Christ could give.

When the appeal was made at the close of that Harvest Service, William was eager to go forward, seeking peace, joy, and satisfaction, in salvation.

For almost half-an-hour Rev. Mc Crea spoke to him, reading with him, praying with him, and explaining to him the simplicity of salvation, and it was then that Linda's father trusted in Christ.

When he came out of the room where he had been talking to the preacher, his face was shining. He had a serenity in his heart he had never known before.

His wife, Louise, hugged him, tears streaming down her face.

They were both unbelievably happy.

The Castles were now united in Christ.

24

JIM

Since the night he was saved when face to face with death in Belfast City Hospital, Chris Killen discovered himself possessed with a new-to-him, and all-consuming passion. As he reflected on the life he had once lived, and how he had more than once knocked on the door of death, and had been spared, Chris wanted to reach out to his former friends. All those young men who were addicted to drink and drugs, and some of whom were fanatical members of paramilitary organizations, needed to hear what had happened to him. And to be told what God could do for them.

The problem was, where, or how, did he begin?

These were the kind of guys who would not take kindly to being preached at by their erstwhile accomplice who had all of a sudden 'turned good living'. And they were certainly not church going types.

An ideal opportunity to make practical meaningful contact with a man whom he knew, and whose brother he had 'run with' for years, came in a telephone call one evening.

A Christian friend phoned him and asked with genuine concern, "Chris, do you remember Jim?"

Chris did remember Jim, but he remembered his brother George, or 'Geordie' as he was known to 'the boys', even better. This 'Geordie' had been a hard man who had seemed to care for nobody, or nothing, but 'the cause'. He also recalled, however, from snippets that 'Geordie' had told him during the days when they had seen one another often, that he and Jim and that whole family had, what Chris now recognized as, a godly, praying mother.

"Well Jim has been shot, and is up in 'The Royal'. They don't know whether he is going to make it or not," his informant went on to complete the picture.

This news came as a challenge to Chris. A man in that situation needed the assurance that only came with faith in Christ. No-one knew that better than Chris. For he had been there.

'I just must go up to visit Jim', was Chris's instant reaction as soon as he had replaced the receiver. But what would he find if he went there? And would he be welcomed? Or chased?

In fear and trembling, Chris prayed, 'Lord, please give me a word for Jim. What do I say to a man like him?'

Then when he began to let the pages of his little Gideon New Testament slide through his fingers, his eye rested on one of the verses he had marked in red, from his skinhead, travels with a machete, days. It was John chapter five, verse twenty-four.

That, thought Chris, is what I will share with Jim.

On arriving in the Hospital ward, Chris discovered that Jim was very ill.

He had been shot five times, and rumour had it that that he had been resuscitated more than once on the operating table. His hours in the operating theatre had literally, critically, been a matter of life and death.

Chris spoke briefly to Jim's father and brother who were sitting numbly, silently, at the shot man's bedside. They were both in a state of profound shock, trying to come to terms with the cold fact that Jim's chances of survival, having sustained multiple gunshot wounds, were very slim. It was that planning-funerals-in-the-mind-but-don't-dare-talk-about-them-yet time for them

Jim lay unconscious, surrounded by tubes, drips and monitors.

When he had asked permission from the two anxious relatives, Chris read his chosen verse, and prayed for Jim.

Then he prepared to leave, for there was little else he could do. Just before turning to face the door Chris asked Jim's father if it would be all right for him to return sometime.

The worried father must have appreciated the absolute sincerity of this Christian visitor for he replied immediately, "No problem. Come back anytime, son. And thank you for your prayer."

Chris did not need a second invitation. He took Jim's father at his word, and began to make regular visits over the next two weeks. And during that period Jim's condition slowly deteriorated. He had been placed on a life support machine and his family and friends became increasingly concerned that there was indeed 'no hope' for him. But they could not just plan the funeral yet either. For he may 'linger another day or two'.

On a Saturday afternoon, at the beginning of Jim's third week in hospital, Chris was driving up to see him again. As he passed Broadway Gospel Hall, a small church building close to the hospital, he noticed the scripture text on the noticeboard at the front. The words on that board struck him with dynamic force. They were the words of the verse he had read in the presence of the unconscious Jim and his concerned relatives just two weeks before. They stood out emblazoned in gold letters on a blue background.

'Verily, verily, I say unto you, He that heareth my word, and believeth on him that sent me, hath everlasting life, and shall not come into condemnation; but is passed from death unto life.'

As Chris read those words and soon made his way up into the car park at 'The Royal', he was beset by an uncanny sense of inner assurance. On two counts.

Firstly, the verse he had been given on the day of his initial visit had been the correct one, and he should use it again.

His second conviction was even more peculiar. Just after he read that text Chris was suddenly persuaded that Jim was going to live. Despite horrendous injuries, a life support machine, and a gloomy prognosis, Jim was not going to die.

The faithful Christian visitor knew, as he entered the hospital door, whether it was by intuition, or divine revelation, or a combination of both, that his prayers for Jim would be answered. He had to be spared, for he had to be saved!

With that affirmation in his heart Chris was somewhat disappointed to find, when he entered the ward, that nothing had changed as far as Jim was concerned. He was still gravely ill, and the grey faced relatives were still maintaining their whispering vigil at his bedside. Nonetheless Chris firmly believed that Jim was going to recover, despite all available evidence seeming to be to the contrary, and so he read John chapter five verse twenty-four again to the small group of solemn, silent, heartbroken relations and prayed more positively for Jim's recovery. His faith did not quite extend to thanking God for his restoration. That would come in time, he was convinced.

So confident had Chris become that Jim would survive, he began to visit him every other day. It would be important to him to witness the miracle of healing which he was so sure was just waiting to happen.

He was not disappointed, either.

By the middle of the next week, much to the relief of the waiting worried family and attentive hospital staff, Jim's condition had begun to show signs of improvement, and by the end of the week he had been taken off the life support machine!

After many months of treatment Jim was discharged from hospital. He would never completely recover from his gunshot wounds, but at least he was alive. One of the shots to his head had rendered him blind, and his body bore the scars of the wounds. It was, though, nothing short of a miracle that he was ever able to go home.

Chris was encouraged by this obvious answer to the prayers of many concerned Christians, and he continued to maintain the contact with Jim. And to pray all the more earnestly for him.

It was hard to believe anything other than that God had spared Jim's life to save his soul.

But could such a thing possibly happen?

25

THE HAVEN

As he walked through the streets of his home town after his conversion, Chris was struck by the number of young people he met who were in exactly the same condition as he had been years before. Many of the decent, upright citizens of Lisburn didn't appreciate the plight of these people, nor did they even realize, some of them, that such a crowd of pleasure-craving young people even existed. Chris, on the other hand, could spot them at once, for he knew the sites and the symptoms. He knew where to look. And what to look for.

Many of these teenagers and young adults lived aimless, pointless lives.

Some of them were drug addicts.

A few of them were alcoholics.

All of them, though, were making valiant efforts to appear satisfied and fulfilled when in reality the were sick-at-heart and frustrated.

Chris could empathize with every single one of them. He knew precisely how they felt. He had been there, where they were, himself. And had lived in that land, the Land of Hollow Happiness, for years.

Something would have to be done for these people. Chris wanted to tell them about what God had done for him, and could do for them. And he did.

Every Friday and Saturday night he returned to the streets and the street-corners he had once frequented. This time, however, he was not secretively hiding a syringe or a precious packet of pills, or openly guzzling the first can of a six-pack of lager with the remaining five in a plastic bag in the other hand, 'for later on'.

No. His essential items of equipment, the basic tools of his trade, were now his Gideon New Testament, tucked away in the hip-pocket of his jeans, for reference if needed, and a batch of appropriate Gospel tracts. These booklets, when offered, to the right person, at the right time, and in the right manner, would often serve to trigger a conversation.

It wasn't long before other members of Lisburn Free Presbyterian Church, recognizing their new member's concern for the youth of the town, offered to help him, and Colin Mc Arthur and Sam McLernon joined him in his stance on the streets.

Every weekend, and occasionally during the week as well, the three men were out, witnessing to their faith in Christ, to all whom they could persuade to listen. Time after time Chris could say, to some mildly interested twenty year-old, or to a group of restless-and-trying-to-appear-resistant teenagers, with complete conviction, and absolute honesty, "I used to stand where you are standing. I once did what you are doing, and I drank, too, what you are drinking. But now I have found satisfaction in another source..." and if they remained long enough, he told them of the miraculous transformation in his life, since trusting in Christ.

The on-the-spot reaction to such bold encounters was much the same as it had been in Bible times, to the presentation of the Gospel. After Paul had addressed an audience of argumentative Greeks on Mars Hill, in Athens, 'some of them mocked, but others said, We will hear you again on this subject.'

That was just how many of those contacted responded to Chris and his companions.

Some mocked. They dismissed the muffled-up men at the corner, with their Gospel handouts in gloved hands, as nut-cases. Weirdos. Cranks.

"Half the trouble in Northern Ireland has been caused by religious fanatics like you boys!" they would jeer.

Others though, were different. They were impressed by what these sincere men, who could just as easily have been sitting in warm homes, at warm fires, had to say, but were unwilling to submit to the claims of Christ in front of their friends at a crowded street-corner. In an attempt to evade the issue, but yet escape with honour, they would procrastinate.

"Come back again some other time, vicar," they would say. "But be sure you make it some time when we are not so cold... or are not so busy...or have more time...or not on our way to a party, or a 'punch-up', or 'the pictures'."

It was what these people said that presented Chris and his friends with the challenge.

Although peppered with short-term and on-the-spur-of-the-moment excuses, their statements also contained an invitation. It was to 'come back again, some other time'. What they really meant was, in effect, 'Don't bother us now. We will hear you again at a later date, and in more congenial circumstances'.

What was needed was a base from which to operate, with an atmosphere in which young people could feel comfortable. A retreat where they could relax. Where they felt confident enough to express their own hopes and fears, or their own personal points of view, without feeling either inhibited or intimidated.

Someone drew the attention of these dedicated street-workers to the fact that the DUP owned a property in Halfpenny Square, Lisburn, which was lying unused at that time.

When they approached Rev. William Beattie of Dunmurry Free Presbyterian Church, who was in charge of that unused office, and stated their case, they were immediately granted use of the rooms, for as long as needed, completely free of charge. This was an answer to prayer, for it was exactly what they knew they needed. It would provide them with an easily accessible centre, right in the centre of town.

There was only one practical problem, however. As the property had lain empty for some time it was in need of some refurbishment. It would have to be thoroughly cleaned, completely re-painted, and then suitably furnished.

It was then that Chris discovered in a very practical way, the wealth of Christian fellowship. He was impressed by the number of people who turned up, armed with all sorts of tools and tins, to offer what assistance they could. Those days of fixing ceilings, painting walls and hanging curtains proved to be profitable for two reasons. The first, and obvious reason was the fact that the place looked so much better, and so much more useable, after they had finished. The other, and perhaps not so immediately recognizable positive outcome of their weeks of often dusty, often demanding, work, was that a camaraderie and sense of vision developed amongst the workers, and many of them offered to help staff the 'drop-in-centre' when it became functional.

At the first meeting of those who had volunteered to help with this work, Rev. William Beattie conducted a dedication service for them. The text he used on that occasion, taken from the story in Luke chapter fourteen, was, 'Go out quickly into the streets and lanes of the city'. These words were immediately adopted by the eager band of let-us-out-and-at-it leaders as their motto, their watchword, their vital source of inspiration. They expressed precisely Chris's vision. To go out to where the needy people were, and to present them with the claims of Christ, in simple language and with lots of love.

The centre was called 'The Haven', for that is what the workers prayed that it would become. A place where souls in search of satisfaction could be given a sympathetic hearing, and share over a cup of tea or coffee, their innermost concerns. The leaders were realistic enough not to expect anything spectacular from the work of 'The Haven', in its initial stages, however. The early days of the work would have to be spent in making contacts, and building confidences, they knew.

Those pioneering days of the work in Halfpenny Square provided the willing volunteers with valuable experience in Christian outreach work. They learnt how to work together, to pray together, to support each other, and how to adapt their approach to the current situation, when dealing with the dozens of different people with their dozens of different problems, who had been invited into the centre, by those of their number who were out scouring the 'streets and lanes' of Lisburn.

It was slow work, requiring constant commitment.

In the early days the discouragements often outweighed the encouragements.

Promising contacts disappeared. Inclement weather occasionally kept everybody indoors at other pursuits. Drunks could be disruptive.

Gradually, though, the name and fame of The Haven spread amongst the would-be-'good-timers' in the community. They came to realize that the helpers there genuinely cared for them, as people, no matter who they were, or where they came from.

The first breakthrough, the first stamp of God's approval on their efforts, as they saw it, came nine months after the opening of The Haven. And it came with Christine. This girl in her late teens began to weep one night, when talking casually across a table to Chris and Linda.

When asked what her problem was Christine replied, "I am afraid."

"Afraid of what?" Linda coaxed, gently.

"I am afraid of death, because I am not ready to die, and I am afraid of hell, for I know, with the life I have lived, that is where I will go to if I die."

When she had finished pouring out her heart to them, Chris continued the conversation. "I know exactly how you feel, Christine, for there was a time when I was terrified of death, as well..." he told her, and then went on to relate the story of his frequent illnesses, the number of times he had been snatched back from the brink of death and hell, and how that fear had now gone completely, since he had trusted Christ.

For more than an hour the three of them talked, with Chris and Linda quoting verses from the Bible to Christine, in an attempt to point her to the Prince of Peace, the only One who could bring her assurance of everlasting life and the consequent quelling of the dread of death.

When the centre closed later that evening, Christine set out for home, with a number of Scripture texts buzzing around in her head, a selection of suitable tracts in her pocket, and a realization in her soul that if she ever wanted to find true peace she needed to be saved.

What she didn't know, though, was that she was being totally surrounded by prayer for her salvation, for the helpers at The Haven had held an impromptu prayer meeting, specifically for her, before they had finally left.

Then, after more than two weeks when Christine, who lived in Belfast, had disappeared from their presence, but not from their prayers, one of the leaders came into the centre all fired-up, "Guess what I have just heard," he enthused, "Christine has got saved at a mission in 'the city'!"

What an encouragement that was! How all those who had struggled to set up a haven of hope on the streets of Lisburn rejoiced! Someone whom they had personally counselled had come into personal contact with Christ.

And that wasn't all.

For Chris there was more.

About six weeks after he had heard of Christine's conversion, Chris had a telephone call from Jim's mother who seemed to reckon she had reason to be pleased. She had just rung, she said, to thank Chris for his prayers and his visits, for Jim, too, had 'just trusted the Saviour', the previous night.

What a thrill!

But what a challenge! God had now demonstrated that He was prepared to use Chris Killen, as a messenger in the effective spread of His gospel.

So what did Chris do now?

Where did he go from here?

26

ENDURE AFFLICTIONS

Chris was happy in The Haven. And happy with it.

The opportunity to spend time with inquisitive teenagers and interested twenty-plus year olds, with an assortment of problems which he well understood, presented him with a challenge which he greatly relished. And when more and more of these young people began to return time after time, bringing a bunch of friends or another batch of pertinent questions with them, he realized that the word of God was beginning to get through to them. Then when others, after Christine, became Christians, Chris was really reassured.

This project had, indeed, been blessed by God.

Chris found himself, over those busy days of preparation for The Haven, and busy days in the work of it, constantly reminded of a verse which he had once read. It had arrested him when he first discovered it, and it influenced him every time he recalled it.

The verse was John chapter nine, and verse four.

The words were the words of Jesus, but both the intention stated, and the urgency implied, impressed Chris. Always.

Jesus told his disciples, in reply to one of their frequent questions, ' I must work the works of him that sent me, while it is yet day : for the night cometh when no man can work.'

That was so true. Nobody realized more than Chris Killen that time on earth, and particularly **his** time on earth, with all his drug-induced physical problems, was limited. And so too was time for some of these people he met week after week. There was a night coming, when the daytime of opportunity, for both him and them, would be over.

Chris became increasingly convinced that the best thing he could do with the rest of his life would be to spend it in some kind of Christian service. There was nothing he could think of that could be more important than trying to see seeking souls saved and ruined lives restored.

The Haven was a wonderful opportunity, but it wasn't a life's work.

There must be something else.

Having given the matter some serious thought, Chris shared his interest in reaching out to others with Dr. John Douglas, Principal of the Whitefield College of The Bible, with a view to commencing a course designed to prepare him for full-time Christian work.

Dr. Douglas advised Chris to give the matter further careful consideration, praying about it over a period of time, and if he still felt that God was leading him to study at the College, to return. Chris did as was suggested, and after several months of prayerful reflection was more convinced than ever that he should enter the College. In September, 1992, Chris was enrolled as a student at The Whitefield College of the Bible. He embarked upon that course with a surge of spiritual enthusiasm burning in his heart, and a niggling natural apprehension chipping away at the back of his mind.

He was thrilled by the course, and with the chance to share experiences and exchange ideas with the others in 'his year'. To have the time to study the Bible in depth under practised yet patient tutors, who had a genuine love for the Word of God, he counted a privilege. And to meet with his fellow-students for prayer in the mornings, before classes began, was a real pleasure.

The College, and the course, were great.

There was only one persistent concern which plagued him constantly. As Chris looked around at the other men who had commenced their studies at the same time as him, they all seemed so fit. So healthy. They had never been as ill as he had. Nor were any of them currently in as poor health as he was.

Chris often thought of those words that Paul had written to Timothy at the end of a long and fruitful life, 'I have finished my course'.

All very well for Paul, Chris mused, but what if I can't finish mine?

Then BANG! it hit him.

He was just congratulating himself at having successfully completed his first year at College, and discussing with Linda, over a period of days in early July, 1993, how they could make best use of the two month summer vacation, when Chris began to feel ill.

In a matter of hours his temperature soared until it was dangerously high. Like a bolt from the blue he was struck by excruciating abdominal pain. He had a severe kidney infection.

His worst-case-scenario had taken place.

Chris was rushed back into Belfast City Hospital. Back to Ward 2 South.

It was devastating.

And just when he was coming along so well, too. The Haven. The College course. The prospect of seeing more souls brought to the Saviour.

Now this. Back to square one. Again.

Was this it? Now? At last?

Here he was, on the brink of death, for the umpteenth time.

Was his life of usefulness over?

Chris struggled with his spiritual problems, despite his absolute physical agony. He was writhing in pain and he felt that his whole body was on fire. There was no respite from either the physical or mental torment.

Verses he had learnt raced through his boiling brain.

At College they had often quoted a verse from Second Timothy, chapter four, usually in relation to preaching or teaching the scriptures. It was,

'But watch thou in all things, endure afflictions, do the work of an evangelist, make full proof of thy ministry.'

Those words came in force to Chris on that hospital bed, but with special emphasis on the two words he had often skipped over before, to get to the preaching and teaching part of the verse. Those two words burned into his brain...

'Endure afflictions...endure afflictions...endure afflictions...'

Well what could be worse than this?

'Endure afflictions...endure afflictions..'.

Well if I can endure this I can endure anything.

'Endure afflictions...'

Yes, Lord, lesson learnt, Chris eventually submitted. I am ready to endure any amount of affliction for You.

Then came the other verse. The one from John chapter nine.

'I must work the works of him that sent me, while it is yet day : the night cometh when no man can work.'

This verse had inspired Chris for the past two years.

Now it came again. Back to him in his bed. In forceful freshness.

In agony of body and soul he cried out in anguish, "Lord, if you heal me now I will work for you for the rest of my life!"

Before entering Bible College, Chris had made a decision to serve God, somehow, somewhere. Now, here, lying in bed, with his life in the balance, he made the commitment.

This was no casual career choice, like, should I be a teacher? Or a nurse perhaps? Or what about a businessman? Maybe even a Christian worker?

No. This was a conscious, long-term, lifetime vow. With body, soul and spirit he cried out to God.

This represented total and absolute commitment.

And within twenty-four hours Chris had 'turned the corner'.

His family, friends and fellow-workers had been praying fervently for him and God had answered their prayers, and with His help and the skill and dedication of the hospital medical staff, the patient's condition began to stabilize. The kidney infection had been checked, the pain had eased, and his temperature had come down.

Chris had been spared, had stepped back from the brink of death, yet again.

Although out of danger, he had to remain in hospital another two weeks, and in those days many people came to visit him. The fellowship with them, and with the man in an adjoining bed, whom Chris discovered was also a Christian, was always uplifting.

This man told Chris one day, after hearing of his impassioned pledge to serve God to the best of his ability, for the remainder of his life, "Son, if God has called you to be a missionary, never stoop to be a king!"

To him, the eternal rewards of Christian service obviously far outweighed any wealth this world could ever offer.

When it was time to be discharged from hospital Chris was told by his consultant that he would have to have daily medical treatment for the rest of his life to keep a very serious internal condition under control. This came as a shock to someone who had just committed himself to serving God with every ounce of his being.

Then he was reminded of the verse which had come so forcibly to him in one of his darkest hours.

'Endure afflictions', it had said. 'Endure afflictions'.

Could this be part of it? Like Paul's 'thorn in the flesh' he wrote about. Something that he wanted to get rid of, but couldn't, and had to suffer throughout all his service?

As Linda was driving Chris back home that day, to salvage for themselves what remained of the summer vacation, the words of a Christian doctor, standing at his bedside, soon after he was saved, flashed back into his mind.

"I am not going to try to explain this condition to you medically, Chris, for I can't," he had counselled, " but now that you have trusted in Christ you will soon discover that you have an adversary, the Devil, who will try to get you down. He will make it his business to hinder your service for God in any way he can. Don't let him defeat you. Just keeping looking to the Lord, for He has conquered the Devil, and He can help you conquer him."

Chris never forgot his last words as he had moved away from the bed, that morning, "Remember, Chris, always look to the Lord, for He alone can see you through!"

In late September, Chris was able to return to commence his second year at Bible College, but from then on he had a difficult time physically, for there were days, and occasionally weeks, at a time, when he was barely able to rise out of bed, without ever considering driving the twenty miles to the College and spending a day in study.

The College authorites, however, were very understanding, recognizing that this young man had both a zeal and an ability to serve God which would not, or could not, be suppressed by his 'often infirmities', and accommodated him in every possible way.

In those days Chris was led to prove, painfully, the true meaning of the two-word message, 'endure afflictions'. Those words had been revealed to him in a moment of physical and spiritual crisis. Now he was being expected to work them out in everyday situations. Day, after day, after day... All the sickness. All the treatment. All the disappointment of not being able to study where and when he wanted. All the doubts dangling about concerning the future. Would he **ever** be able to serve God effectively, a fervid soul in a feeble body?

Life was not going to be any 'bed of roses' for him. Christians all down the ages had been called upon to 'endure afflictions'. Many had suffered hunger and thirst, sickness and sorrow, loneliness and homelessness for the sake of their Saviour.

Indeed many had laid down their lives. As martyrs for the Master.

So why should he complain? Or expect to be any different?

Despite all the hardships and setbacks, however, Chris was often encouraged by the doctor's personal prophecies.

Yes. He had experienced at close-quarters the Devil and his desire to disrupt.

But he had also experienced, in a very real way, the truth of the prediction that 'if you look to the Lord, He alone will see you through'.

God had both the Almighty power in heaven, and the available personnel on earth, to see him through those next two years at College.

And through the rest of his life as well.

27

LIFE IN THE LIGHTHOUSE

Chris graduated from the Whitefield College of the Bible in June 1995, feeling that he was at least partially prepared for a life of service for his Lord. What he now needed was an on-the-ground opportunity to put all the theory into practice. See how it worked out in a real-life situation.

The three year course had been both instructive and inspirational, but Chris now needed to find out how he could make the best use of his time, his experience, and his training, in the implementation of his impassioned promise to work for his Lord for the rest of his life.

He had never felt called to be a preacher. For one thing, his haphazard health meant that he would find it impossible to undertake the sundry, and often stressful, duties of a church ministry, but also he felt that his forte lay in one-to-one contacts with boys like he had been. Drug-addicts, drunkards, drop-outs.

It was during his final term at College that Chris heard about 'The Lighthouse'.

This was a centre run by somebody called 'Joseph' in Pearse Street, Dublin. And it sounded like the sort of place where Chris would feel at home. An outreach drop-in centre for Dublin's 'druggies'. The 'Haven' on a more regular basis, and serving a much wider population with more complex problems.

Chris contacted 'Joe' at 'The Lighthouse' and arranged a preliminary, fact-finding visit, and his first impression was that this was the ideal set-up for him.

This was exactly his kind of place. And these were exactly his kind of people.

After some consultation Chris arranged to spend two days every week working in the centre. This would be an ideal place 'to serve his apprenticeship' in the work to which he was sure that God had called him, and for which his past life had practically, but painfully, equipped him. Reaching people with problems personally for the Lord.

Lighthouses are located in strategic positions around our shores, with the express purpose to warn of danger, and their method of achieving this aim is to shoot a shaft of stabbing light through the blackest night.

Chris hadn't been long working in the Dublin 'Lighthouse' until he discovered the strategic nature of its location. It had been opened right beside a methadone clinic for heroin addicts. It was so positioned that it could shine its life-enhancing light through the gathering gloom.

The centre opened from ten o'clock every morning until two o'clock every afternoon, and 'Joe' and his 'lighthouse keepers' offered tea or coffee and toasted sandwiches, at minimal cost and all served with compassion, to those who chose to call in.

Although the light refreshments were always welcomed by the often cold and usually hungry visitors to the centre, caring Christian leaders had more to offer them than hot drinks and welcome food.

They took every opportunity possible to tell of the One who loved them, Who had come to earth to die for them, and Who could turn their lives around in a remarkable way, just as he had done for Joe, and Chris, and some of the others.

Joe told Chris that he believed these people could 'be loved to the Lord.' They hadn't come in to be preached at, they had come in seeking comfort, consolation, and peace, both in body and soul. It was that quest for ultimate satisfaction that had led to their beginning to dabble in drugs in the first place, and they had to be shown that lasting satisfaction of the soul could only be found through faith in Christ.

And 'Joe' had developed a novel approach in the Lighthouse to making sure that these people were presented with that message.

"There's a verse in the Bible, Chris," he explained his philosophy to his understudy one day, "and it says that 'faith comes by hearing, and hearing by the word of God'. We are trying to teach these people the word of God, and then hope that this will either give us the chance to talk to them about the Gospel, or perhaps it may even lead them to the Lord themselves."

And his method of teaching the 'word of God' was also appropriately innovative.

The walls of the Lighthouse were lined with attractive scripture text posters, all chosen to point the reader to the person of Christ. They were some of the declarations of Jesus about himself. The 'I AM's' of the Gospels.

'I AM the door: by me if any man enter in, he shall be saved...'

'I AM the good shepherd: the good shepherd gives his life for the sheep...'

'I AM the way, the truth and the life: no man comes to the Father, except through me...'

In a prominent position was a colouful poster of a lighthouse, its bright beams spreading out in all directions, and proclaiming the message, 'I AM the light of the world: whoever follows me will never walk in darkness, but will have the light of life'.

The deal was that if any of the addicts or others who had called into the centre could learn, and repeat, one of these verses, they were given a free cup of tea or coffee. It sounded rather simple, but some of the folks whose vision or thinking or both had been impaired by the persistent use of drugs, or others who had learning difficulties, found it quite a challenge, and were consequently rather pleased to achieve it. And earn a free hot drink. The leaders at the Lighthouse were also pleased on these occasions for it was another 'entrance' of the word of God. And in a verse they often quoted, 'the entrance of thy word giveth light'.

The light of God from His Pearse Street 'Lighthouse'.

During his year of working in the Lighthouse Chris saw many sad and empty people struggling along in many sad and empty situations but he witnessed the plight of one particular person, and stood in one particular place, and each of these experiences, in its own way, made an indelible impression on him.

The first happened in the Lighthouse.

It had been a normal day, in so far as there ever was such a thing as 'a normal day', when every day seemed to present its own set of challenges, when Chris noticed a young woman in the corner, whom he had never seen before. She looked to be in her late teens. Perhaps maybe eighteen.

It was her appearance that held Chris's attention. She looked wretched. Her breathing was coming in short, shallow gasps. There was a hollow, hopeless look in her sunken eyes.

"What's the matter with that girl over there, Joe?" Chris enquired in a slack moment. He felt so sorry for her.

"That girl has aids," Joe replied sympathetically when he was sure he understood who it was that Chris meant. "Some of the people who come in here have tested HIV positive, but she has full-blown aids."

"Is there any hope for her?" Chris wanted to know. Her case certainly didn't appear too hopeful.

"No. I doubt there isn't," Joe went on seriously.

"You mean to tell me that she will probably die of aids?" Chris was almost overcome. He had seen some desperate cases before on the streets of both Belfast and London, but never anything quite so pathetic as this.

Joe thought for a moment before replying, then continued, his voice soft and low, "Yes and No, Chris. She is probably going to die, but it won't be of aids. She will die of loneliness. The loneliness and hopelessness that have driven her into this situation."

The last sighting Chris had of that girl was in the afternoon, about two-thirty. Joe and he had just tidied up the centre after that day's activity, had prepared it for the next, and had stepped outside. Joe was in the process of securing the front door when Chris saw her again.

There she was, sitting forlornly on the steps, her head in her hands. Her unkempt hair fell loosely over her bony shoulders.

As they descended the steps, on their way home for the evening and night, Joe bent down and spoke to her. It was a statement, made to sound like a question.

"See you again tomorrow, Mary?"(not her real name)

'Mary' never moved. Just shook her head.

And they didn't see her 'again tomorrow'.

Or the next day. Or the next.

In fact 'Mary' never came back.

They were never to see her again...

The other Dublin experience which made a lasting impression on Chris happened just before Christmas.

On a dark December day, just as they were locking up The Lighthouse again, Joe asked Chris if he was 'in a big hurry home'. When Chris replied that he wasn't 'really', Joe went on to say, "That's good for I have something to show you."

After they had driven through a few streets they arrived at the 'something' Joe had to show his friend. This 'something' turned out to be a Christmas tree, almost sixty feet tall, which had been set up in Mc Dermott Street.

The unique feature about this particular Christmas tree, as Chris was soon to discover, was the way in which it had been decorated. The tree had been lined with sparkling tinsel from top to bottom, as had all the other similar trees in the city. But that was where the similarity ended. For instead of balloons and bells and brightly-wrapped bogus parcels, that tree had been hung with photographs. Chris was sure there must have been at least one hundred of them, all laminated against the winter weather.

He was puzzled.

"What's the meaning of all this Joe?" was the immediate question on his lips.

Again Joe looked serious. And it was no wonder, for the message he had to convey, about 'the meaning of all this', was a serious one.

"Every photograph you see on that tree," he went on to explain, "is of somebody from this area of Dublin who has died from drug abuse. Their parents and friends put up this tree every year to highlight the problem."

Again Chris was stunned. He stepped forward and looked at some of the pictures near ground level. There were photos there of intelligent looking teenagers in school uniforms...of tough-looking characters...of university graduates in their gowns...of mere children...

The whole spectrum of young society was represented.

All these, Joe had said, were the people from this area of Dublin alone, who had died from drug abuse.

It was shocking. Chris had never realized that the drug problem in Ireland's largest city was so acute.

He stayed for almost an hour at that tree, walking around, looking at the pictures, thinking of the parents and friends who had supplied them, with aching, breaking hearts...

His year in The Lighthouse, and especially the abject hopelessness of 'Mary', and the pathos of the picture Christmas tree, made Chris more determined than ever to do all that he could, for as long as God spared him the health, to help such people.

He would strive to bring the message of the Gospel, the only true source of hope and light and life and love to them.

But where? Or how?

28

THE OPEN DOOR

In the early autumn of 1996 Chris became a father again.

What a difference though, this time from last.

When Samantha was born Chris had been so ill from the effects of his addictions that he had attempted to take his own life. Now he was saved, settled, and satisfied, and he and Linda were delighted that God had given them the gift of a second daughter on 13th October.

Not surprisingly, they called her Grace.

It was a tremendous joy also for Samantha, who was then ten years old, to have a little baby sister to look after.

Everybody was so happy. So thrilled. And so fulfilled.

Chris was still working on the streets of Lisburn and Belfast, contacting alcoholics and drug addicts, trying to show Christian love and care to desperate souls in sad situations. And in urgent need of salvation.

He wanted, though, to establish this as his life's work. With every night out, and every contact made, he became more convinced that this was what he wanted to do for his Lord. For the rest of his life. On a more permanent, structured, recognized, basis.

In an attempt to seek support for his vision Chris met the Mission Board of the Free Presbyterian Church on Tuesday, 5th November, 1996. He explained to them how he felt that God was leading him into full-time service as a missionary, as his health would permit.

The only difference between this interview, and others which the Mission Board had previously conducted, was that this particular applicant didn't want to serve the Lord in some far away place like Latvia or Luxembourg. But in Lisburn.

Not in Brazil or Bangladesh, but in Belfast or Ballymena.

Chris wanted to present the Gospel of God's saving grace to the addicts in his own province. His mission field, as he envisaged it, would not be in some foreign country, but amongst a specific sector of society, with whom he could readily relate, in his own country.

This, for the Mission Board, was a novel request. Yet they were sympathetic.

They felt, however, that they needed more time to consider such a different, but nonetheless definite, and potentially productive, application, and they obviously felt that Chris did too. So they suggested that he 'go away and pray about it'. This sounded like one of those put-you-off excuses. Another 'come-back-when-you're-ready' job. Like parents telling their little ones that 'you can do that sort of thing when you grow up'. But they assured him it wasn't.

The Board weren't saying 'No'. They were just saying, 'Wait. 'Pause'. 'Ponder'.

And Chris did as they had asked. He went away.

Continued to work. And continued to pray.

Then, almost a year later, in August 1997, as Chris was driving along in the car, listening to the tape of a sermon by Rev. Alan Cairns, which had been recorded in Ballymoney Free Presbyterian Church some years before, he was tremendously challenged by the message.

Rev. Cairns had been conducting a series of teaching meetings on 'The Seven Churches in Asia' from the early chapters of the Bible book of Revelation.

The tape Chris happened to be listening to was about chapter three. And the church in Philadelphia.

As the words of the preacher thundered out of the speakers in the car, Chris found himself transfixed. Left driving along in a kind of a daze...

"There are people in this meeting, and before you stands an open door. Perhaps you are a Christian and it is an open door to service. Fear not to go in, my friend.

Take your stand for God.

Go in through that door.

And God will be with you.

And the Christ of God will bless you.

And the Spirit of God will strengthen you.

And not all the devils in hell or out of hell will be able to overcome you.

For when HE opens the door, nobody will shut it in your face..."

There was a momentary pause as the preacher prepared to present the alternative. He then continued, in relatively muted tones, 'But if you DON'T go in, and God shuts the door, you will pray 'God give me the chance to go in'...But it will be lost forever..."

That spoke to Chris. Three phrases from the sermon struck him.

'An open door to service'...'the chance to go in'... 'lost forever'.

He could hardly wait to get home and sit down with his precious Gideon New Testament. Turning hastily to Revelation chapter three he skimmed down the verses looking for the one about the open door. It didn't take him long to find it, for it wasn't far down the chapter.

It was verse eight...

'I know thy works : behold, I have set before thee an open door, and no man can shut it : for thou hast a little strength, and hast kept my word, and hast not denied my name...'

Chris read it over to himself a few times, and as he did he noticed words that he could not remember ever having heard before. And if he had ever heard them before they certainly had never stuck him with such force as they did that evening.

'For thou hast a little strength...'

That was what had been holding him back from returning to the Mission Board. He had spent more than nine months now, working away with people like the person he once had been. People who were destroying themselves, body, mind and soul with drink and drugs.

But his health was his problem. He had told the Mission Board that he wanted to be a missionary, as his health would permit. After all, had he not been told that he would be on strong medication every day for the rest of his life, just to keep him alive?

He had just 'a little strength'.

But he HAD 'a little strength'.

There was, too, a door 'wide open' right in front of him, and it was a special door that only he could go through. It was an open door into a shady domain. It led into the realm of alcohol and amphetamines. Of morphine and heroin. Of cannabis and cocaine. Of addiction, depression, and early tragic death...

And many of these people had never even heard of the Saviour who could save them from both physical and spiritual disaster. Pull them back from the brink. Where he had been. So often.

News of his interest in this particular field had spread around his home town and was gradually beginning to creep, like the gentle tide of a flat calm sea up a flat sunlit shore, across other counties as well. He was being asked to address pupils in schools and young people in youth organizations, in an increasing number of places, about the dangers of drugs.

Then recently there had been that query from an adult group, too.

'Would Chris be interested in coming along to tell us something about the drugs problem, and what are the signs of an involvement with drugs? We are concerned about our teenage children.'

The open door was now hard back against the wall. It couldn't open any wider.

Chris had a little strength. And he would use it. If he could, and as much as he could, for as long as he could.

In late August he approached the Mission Board again. He had 'gone away' and had 'prayed about it'. Long and hard. And now he was back.

He was invited to attend a meeting of the Board on Tuesday, 7th October, 1997, and at that meeting he told the members about the tape in the car, the open door, his little strength, the openings to speak about drugs, and the opportunities to contact people in various stages of drug involvement, with the life and light of the Gospel.

The Board were convinced.

At that meeting Chris Killen was accepted as a missionary, working specifically in the area of drug abuse.

He had entered through the open door.

For God. Who had opened it.

And if HE had opened it, no man could shut it.

Or so the Bible, and the teacher-on-the-tape, had said.

29

SO WHAT IS A DRUG?

The door was open.

Chris had stepped in through it in the firm belief that God had told him to, convinced that he was about to enter a whole new realm of challenge. And opportunity.

Now all that he needed were some new gates, into some new fields, where he could be useful to God, and helpful to others in need.

It wasn't long, either, until God gave him his chance. When he was invited to speak to pupils in a drugs awareness class in a large secondary school in County Armagh, he gladly accepted.

Then he spent the next two weeks before the lesson worrying, wondering, preparing.

This was just what he had wanted. Just what he had believed himself equipped to do. To speak to vulnerable teenagers about the dangers of drug abuse.

But what had he let himself in for?

He was not a teacher, just a converted addict who had once been expelled from school in his teens.

How could he possibly address a class? And sound credible?

As the pre-arranged date approached Chris became increasingly nervous about this, his first school meeting.

He thought much, and prayed even more, about it. Surely the God who had opened the door for him to do this, wouldn't desert him now.

And He didn't.

When the day came Chris was ushered into a crowded classroom. There seemed to be about forty teenagers, both boys and girls, in that room. There were so many of them. Perhaps two classes had been amalgamated to hear what this 'drugs expert' had to say.

What if they started to ask him all sorts of awkward questions? How would he cope?

It was intimidating at first. His trust though, was still in God, and in God alone.

Chris had spent the most of the previous night awake, tossing and turning and talking to his Heavenly Father, about precisely that very moment.

When it came his turn to stand up before the pupils Chris was enveloped by a strange sense of calm. He was about to open his mouth, and God had promised to fill it.

He began with a personal introduction, explaining why he considered himself qualified to speak on the subject.

"I was once a drug addict," he told them, gaining confidence by the second from the obvious interest of his teenage audience. "When I was just a little older than you people here today I became a skinhead and an addict, was involved in many unpleasant practices, and ended up nearly wrecking my life. Then when I was twenty-three I became a Christian and discovered that to be the answer to all my needs and cravings. I learnt, too, that all I needed to know about anything, including my attitude to drugs, is to be found in the Bible."

Having established himself as someone who wished to pursue this subject from a Christian perspective, he continued, "I believe that God has created all of our bodies, and that He has created them to work in a very special way. He has designed them to run on a special kind of fuel, called food and drink.."

Chris then paused to ask a question to stimulate thought, and put his point across. "I have a friend who has a diesel car," he went on. "What do you think happened one day when he made a mistake at a filling-station and put petrol into it?"

A shower of hands shot up and a shower of smiles shot across many faces. By the show of knowing smirks, probably some of the audience had parents or friends who had done that very same thing!

"Well what happened?" Chris probed, pointing to a lad in the second row.

"It didn't go!" he replied, with a laugh.

"That's right," the questioner was pleased, for he had been given the response he expected. "In fact it did go. For about two hundred yards, and then it spluttered and stopped. You see its engine wasn't designed to run on that kind of fuel. It gummed up all its works."

Having made that point Chris changed his tack. He had laid the foundation for his talk. Now he had to begin building on it.

"I have another question to ask you," he told them. "What is a drug?"

There was a short, incredulous silence, as though the pupils were offended at being asked such a simple question. A few people volunteered to answer.

"It's a sort of a powder," somebody said.

"It's tablets," somebody said.

"It's stuff that's bad for you," somebody said.

"Drugs are dangerous," came from somebody else.

Chris took her up on that one.

"Now hold on a minute there," he retorted, gently. "Think about that for a moment. Are ALL drugs dangerous? What about penicillin? And a whole range of antibiotics?"

The girl who had given the 'drugs are dangerous' answer smiled shyly. She had never thought of that.

"Some drugs are helpful, and necessary," Chris explained. "Millions of people across the world, including myself, would die without drugs. So let me tell you what I think a drug is."

He then went over to the blackboard, which he had been told he could use, and wrote out his definition of a drug in scrawly script which climbed up the board from left to right at a thirty degree angle.

'A drug is any chemical substance which alters the way the body works' was the message.

When he had allowed his audience to read his blackboard description Chris endeavoured to further direct their minds towards his ultimate aim.

"You can all now appreciate, I think, that there are two kinds of drugs. Useful, helpful drugs, and dangerous harmful drugs, but they will all, when taken, alter the way your body works. With prescribed and medicinal drugs this is for our good, but with other drugs it can do our bodies all sorts of damage. Our bodies are not made to cope with them. They are the wrong kind of fuel."

Chris had now taken confidently to his task. It was going well. God was guiding.

"We want now to focus on what are termed the dangerous drugs," he continued. "What do you think they are?"

There was a rapid response to that question. Many hands were up. Many thought they knew.

As Chris stood at the blackboard, he wrote down all the answers as they came flying forward, "Ecstasy"... "Heroin"... "Cocaine"... "Crack"... "Speed"... "Cannabis"...

Slowly, as all the well-known names were lined down the blackboard, in a higgledy-piggledy list beside and around the cockeyed definition, the supply of information from the rows of desks began to dry up.

"Is that all?" Chris coaxed. "Are there no more?"

Rows of blank, bewildered faces gazed back at him.

They thought they had done well. The blackboard was almost covered in large looped letters.

"What about alcohol and tobacco then? Are they not drugs, too?" Chris suggested.

The response to that idea was only half-hearted.

Obviously no-one had ever thought of them as additions to the list of harmful-cum-dangerous drugs.

"Tobacco and alcohol are what some people call soft drugs," Chris proceeded to explain, "yet because they are legal does not necessarily mean they are harmless. Did you know, for instance that there are over four thousand chemicals in tobacco, and more than two hundred of these are highly poisonous? Smoking can have just as damaging, if not just as sudden, consequences for people's health, as using some other drugs."

He then spent the next twenty minutes detailing each type of drug, and its particular effects. For each of them he was extremely careful to point out the attendant dangers, which are sometimes not readily recognized.

When his period was almost up, Chris summarized his underlying message.

"Really what I have been saying to you this afternoon is that taking drugs is a bit like obtaining goods on hire purchase. You take now and pay later. The Bible says that if you sow the wind you will reap the whirlwind. Whether a drug takes twenty years to kill you, or just two minutes, it makes no difference. Your health and indeed your life are too precious to mess about with. Take a bit of advice from me, from somebody who nearly killed himself on drugs, 'If you are dabbling in drugs, stop. And if you are tempted to dabble, don't. Look after your body. It is the one the Creator gave you. And it is the only one you have, and the only one you are going to get...'"

As he drove home later on that afternoon Chris thought back to another afternoon when he had been driving along, listening to a tape. About an open door.

God had opened a very practical door to him in a school that day, and he had gone through it. He felt satisfied that he had been to some degree successful in warning those young people about the dangers of dabbling in drugs. And if only one person had been warned off it would have been an answer to prayer and a compensation for all the preparation. Hopefully there may have been even more than one.

Prevention, he told himself, was better than cure.

It had definitely been a worthwhile exercise.

And it was only the start.

30

HOW WOULD I KNOW? WHAT SHOULD I DO?

A further opportunity to speak about the problems and dangers of drug abuse to a different target audience, with a different perspective on the problem, opened up for Chris on Monday, 28th September, 1998.

A special meeting had been arranged in The Jesus Saves Mission Church in Belfast at which it had been advertised that he would address a group of parents drawn from the immediate neighbourhood about drugs awareness. Prior to the meeting Chris and a number of the local church leaders visited homes in the district inviting parents particularly to attend.

When it came to the night of the meeting the attendance was not as large as the organizers had expected. They were encouraged, however, by the fact that there were some people in that night who had never been inside that church, or perhaps had never been inside any church, in their lives, before.

It was obvious that there were at least some anxious parents in the local community. Parents who had questions about drugs and concerns about sons and daughters and drugs. These people found the invitation to hear what a converted addict turned full-time-drugs-awareness-worker had to say, hard to refuse.

There was an expectant hush as Chris mounted the platform.

This, for him, was a tremendous challenge.

He had a dual purpose in speaking to those parents that evening.

His first objective was to make them aware of some facts in relation to the growing drugs problem in their city, and how that very problem could possibly have crept into their own homes. More importantly, though, he considered it vital that they should have explained to them the underlying cause of the problem, sin, and its only solution, salvation.

When he had introduced himself in his usual way, Chris began his talk with the simple question, 'Why do young people take drugs?'

This was something many of the parents present had often wondered about. 'Why would healthy, and apparently happy, young people want to do it anyway?'

There are many, many reasons, any one of which, or any combination of which, lead young people, and especially teenagers, to experiment with drug-taking.

A few of these Chris chose to outline, as follows,

'**Peer Pressure**. If my friends do it I must do it too. I can't be seen to be left out, or a coward. A chicken.

Curiosity. They have heard so much about it that they want to experience the sensations for themselves.

Escape. Life has so many problems, particularly in adolescence, that drug-taking appears to afford an escape from the real world.

Pleasure. There is a perception that if you take drugs, life will be all one big, long, happy 'high'. 'On cloud nine' all the time.' This is not the case. The Bible states that the 'pleasures of sin' just last 'for a season'. There may be brief pleasure in drug-taking, but there is no permanent satisfaction.'

After he had given the crowd of interested parents these examples of the reasons why young people became involved with drugs to begin with, Chris continued to explain the deeper, more fundamental, cause.

"What I have told you already are only symptoms of a basic, common condition," he went on to say. "This condition is called sin. When God created man, the Bible tells us that He created him in his own image so that God could enjoy communion with him, the Creator with His creation. When Adam sinned in the Garden of Eden that fellowship was broken, and that is why people take drugs, shoot people, burn cars, rob houses and so on. These people, in fact all people, are born in sin and this sin has separated them from God. Taking drugs is an attempt they make to obtain satisfaction, but drugs are only a substitute for the real thing. The real life. A life lived in contact with God."

Sensing the need to revert to his main theme, Chris went on, "There are three levels of drug abuse in society.

Level one is **Experimental.** Your son or daughter might be going through a phase of dipping into drugs, possibly as a result of peer pressure.

Level two is **Recreational**. With this user there is a pattern of occasional use and abuse. For example, at the weekends only.

Level three is the most dangerous level, and the most difficult to deal with. For level three is **Dependent**. And unfortunately there is a progression. Experimental can lead through recreational to dependent, if not caught and checked.

The weekend drinker never intended to become an alcoholic.

But he did.

The girl who had a shot of heroin, 'just for a laugh', never intended to become a 'junkie'.

But she did."

He then further illustrated practically how an experimental dabbler can easily become an incurable addict, by inviting his audience to try winding a piece of thread round and round two fingers, sometime, until they find it impossible to move them, to break free from the bond.

Aware that his audience had come to hear something about the drugs problem, Chris proceeded to describe for them all the different types of drugs, available, on the streets, to their children, as follows.

'Drugs can be divided into four groups.

1. **Depressants.** These drugs slow down the brain and the functions of the body.

Examples of depressants would be,

(a) Alcohol. The first mention of alcohol in the Bible comes in the story of Noah, where it is associated with sin and a curse, and it has been a blight on society ever since.

(b) Cannabis.

(c) Tablets. Sleeping tablets, valium, librium

(d) Solvents. These are very dangerous and unpredictable.

2. **Stimulants.** These drugs act in the opposite way to depressants. They actually speed up the way the brain works and sends its messages to various parts of the body. Examples are, speed, cocaine and crack.

3. **Hallucinogenics**. These can alter the way a person sees things, such as light and colour. They can cause hallucinations. Examples are LSD and 'Magic Mushrooms'. These drugs have a powerful effect upon the mind. The Bible says again that 'the god of this world hath blinded the minds of them that believe not, lest the light of the glorious gospel of Christ, who is the image of God, should shine unto them.' The devil blinds the minds of people. And the use of drugs is one very convenient way he has of doing it.

Ecstasy falls into two categories for it is a stimulant with hallucinogenic effects. It causes the heart to speed up and raises blood pressure, and can have devastating side-effects.

4. **Opiates.** These are the drugs which can be used to reduce pain. Best known examples are heroin and morphine. Heroin is a powder obtained from the opium poppy, and is either smoked or injected. Very few people come off heroin successfully because of the major psychological barriers which have to be overcome...'

Everyone in the Church had listened intently as Chris had specified for them all the different types of drugs available to their growing children, and their expected and supposedly pleasant effects and their unexpected and definitely unpleasant side-effects.

Many were amazed at the scale of the problem. They just had no idea what was going on in their streets, possibly on their own doorsteps.

"Normally at the end of a meeting like this," Chris went on, "we would leave time for you to ask me questions, but as our time is running out, I am now going to ask, and then answer, the two questions you were going to ask me anyway." This was said with a faint smile, for every time he had invited questions after such a gathering, he had been confronted with these two.

"The first thing you are sitting there wanting to ask me is, 'How would I know if my son or daughter was taking drugs?'"

From the nods of approval in the congregation Chris knew that he had struck a chord. He had been spot on in his assumption. So he followed up quickly.

"There are a variety of signs, any combination of which will give you a fair idea that your child is at least experimenting with drugs.

The first, and most obvious of these is usually **a change in behaviour**. Look out for a change in attitude or appearance, for unpredictable mood swings, or the sudden and unexplained possession of large amounts of money, for instance.

Your suspicions should also be aroused by certain particular **physical signs**, which could be dilated eyes, slurred speech, memory lapses or spots around the mouth.

Another tell-tale sign can be **a dramatic deterioration in school performance**. Questions need to be asked when a son or daughter, who has regularly been scoring 'B' or 'C' in his or her progress tests, suddenly, or perhaps even gradually over a period of time, starts to come home with a regular string of 'E's and 'F's.

Probably the sign which every parent dreads discovering, is the actual **possession of drugs or paraphernalia**, like pipes, rolling papers, pills or needles."

A sea of concerned faces gazed up at Chris. Some of the parents there were beginning to worry about certain of those signs they had seen. One mother's mind immediately turned to Harry who had been so hard to work with lately, always moody, unusually withdrawn. Another parent had her Sally whose monthly progress reports from school were becoming steadily worse, and they shouldn't either, for she was such 'a bright wee girl'...

Recognizing the mental anguish that the outlining of such a list of possible signs could cause, Chris hurried on to his next question. The second one that he was invariably asked at such meetings.

"The next thing you will want to know is, "If I think my child is involved in drug taking in some way, what should I do about it?"

Again he had 'hit the nail on the head'. Again there were the nods of agreement. Again the smiles of encouragement and yet urgency. They were saying in effect, 'Yes. That's right. Hurry up and get on with it!'

"Every young person is different. So is every parent. And every family. Thus every situation can require some differences in approach, but there are a number of steps that any worried parent can take in this situation," the speaker assured his intently interested audience.

"The first is to **seek help**. We are here tonight to offer help. We will talk to you about your concerns for your children, and give what advice we can. That is why we have arranged this meeting, so that we can be of some help to you.

Alternatively, if you do not want to speak to someone here, you could seek medical advice. Your doctor can put you in touch with support organizations like the CAT (Community Addiction Teams). Or your local church might have a support or advice group. But the important thing is to seek help from somebody!

The most vital piece of advice that I give to every group that I speak to is, if you are a Christian, **pray**. When I was at my worst, although I hadn't a clue about it, my mother and a number of other desperately concerned Christians were praying for me. And if God hadn't answered those prayers I am quite sure I wouldn't be standing here before you today. I would be dead, no doubt about it!

And what if you are not a Christian? The message for you is that you should get saved, get right with God, and then pray. You will remember that I talked at the start about sin, and how that sin had separated us all from God. In fact the Bible says that 'All have sinned, and come short of the glory of God.'

There is a way back to God, though. Our Lord Jesus Christ came into the world, to die on the cross to take away the punishment for our sins, and the Bible, which presents for us the problem of sin also provides for us the solution in salvation. 'Believe on the Lord Jesus Christ and thou shalt be saved,' it says.

That is the priority for you. Trust in Christ tonight and be saved, and then pray to Him for your family...'

Time was up. Chris felt satisfied. Again it had gone well.

Before stepping down from the platform he renewed the offer of help he had made earlier, for he was convinced that there were a number of genuinely concerned parents in the congregation.

"I am not rushing away now," he told them. " I will be around here for some time to come. If you are worried about anything please feel free to come and talk to me."

He never knew what would happen when he made such an offer. There were times when two or three people had hung around behind to speak to him. At other times the church had cleared like in a bomb scare, and he had spoken to nobody.

Time would tell what would happen that night...

31

THE BANG, AND THE BUMP
IN THE BATHROOM

As many of the congregation filed out past Chris and into the early autumn night, they shook his hand heartily and told him how much they had 'enjoyed that.'

When he was sure that all the people who wanted to go out had gone out, he began to thread his way slowly back up through those who were obviously in no hurry home. He was going to pick up his Bible and notes and then make for Lisburn, himself.

It was then that he noticed a woman, probably a mother, with a boy, probably her son, half-leaning, half-standing, half-sitting, on or against the seats at the end of a row.

The woman appeared to be in her mid-thirties and also appeared to be rather upset.

The boy was about ten or eleven, Chris reckoned, and seemed far from happy.

As he drew up alongside them, the woman spoke.

"Could I have a word with you?" she enquired, anxiously.

"Of course you can," Chris replied warmly. "That is what I asked you to do. That's what I am here for."

Some, but only some, of the pressure, faded from her pained expression.

"I want to speak to you about my son here," the mother went on. "I am really worried about him."

The boy gazed down at the floor. Then up at the ceiling. Then over at the back wall. All with an air of disdain. He was trying to appear disinterested. And disgusted.

Completely ignoring her son's attention-seeking-tactics, Chris addressed his mother.

"Certainly, what about him?" he asked.

"Well, I mean, what I want to know is," she began, seeming unsure of how to say whatever it was she wanted to say.

Then she came out with it.

"Are those solvents, as you call them, really as dangerous as you make them out to be?" she blurted out, all in a gush.

"Yes, I'm afraid they are," Chris told her, calmly, confidently. "Why?"

"Well about a week ago this boy here spent a long time in our bathroom one night. As the bathroom is just up above our kitchen, and I could hear no noise coming from it I was just about to yell up and ask him what he was at when I heard a sharp bang and then a muffled bump," the mother explained, her sentences tripping into each other. She was obviously so pleased to be able to open up to somebody about it.

Then, totally disregarding the son who was trying to totally disregard her, she carried on with her story.

"I ran upstairs and luckily the lock on the bathroom door was broken. When I burst in I found him in a heap on the floor. There was a can beside him and an awful smell. He had a big red mark on the side of his head. The bang had been him hitting the edge of the bath on the way down. The bump had been him hitting the floor."

Son was beginning to feel increasingly awkward. And look increasingly agitated.

"I panicked," his mother continued. "Didn't know what to do. So I threw water over him and in about five minutes he came round."

Then, breaking off, she looked distractedly across in the direction of her son, who by this time had his back on her.

"Please mister will you speak to him?" she begged, turning her attention back to the only person who appeared interested in her problem.

"Yes, I think I should," Chris replied at once, the earnestness of his response engendered from a combination of the mother's distress and the son's danger.

Rather reluctantly the boy accepted Chris's invitation to 'sit down here until we have a chat for a minute or two.'

When they were sitting side by side, with mother on son's other side, Chris said, "I don't think you know the danger you are putting yourself in sniffing solvents."

"I don't believe you that it is all THAT dangerous!" the boy retorted cheekily. At least that was some sort of a breakthrough. Those were the first words he had spoken.

"It is a very dangerous game you were at," Chris told him. "Sniffing solvents gives you an instant high. You feel great at the time. But then they slow down your brain, and your body. That's what happened to you in the bathroom. You were a lucky lad that you didn't kill yourself!"

Son had become suitably subdued.

Not waiting for him to make some other contradictory comment, Chris pursued his point. "Think back to that short video clip I showed you when I was talking earlier on. Do you remember the picture of the Christmas tree? Well, some of those kids there were only ten years old. And they died doing what you were doing in the bathroom."

Satisfied that he was at last being listened to, Chris decided to ask this now much more chastened young chap a question. There was something he always wanted to know from people like this. The information gleaned from such questionings he hoped to be able to use in the education of others.

"Where did you learn to sniff?" he enquired. "Who told you about it?"

There was a moment or two's silence and Chris thought that he had lost it. This character isn't going to answer me at all, he thought. But he was wrong.

"Nobody taught me about it. Or told me about it. I just knew how to do it," he retorted, eventually.

Chris looked across at him sideways, a cynical smile playing around the edges of his lips. "Come on now, son. Do you think I'm daft or somethin'?" he goaded him. "Do you honestly think that I believe you just wakened up one morning and said to yourself, 'Great idea I will sniff some solvent today'? No way! Somebody, somewhere, told you!"

It was the ten year old's turn to give a wry smile. He realized he wasn't going to 'pull the wool over this man's eyes'.

There was another pause.

Was he going to respond to that?

He did, at last, and when he did, it was with a totally different attitude than he had previously demonstrated.

"I learnt it from my friends," he confessed, meekly. "Most of my friends are at it. And an awful lot of the boys in my class."

What a statement! And what an eye-opener for Chris.

"That is terrible!" he replied, shocked. "Terrible!"

Then he returned to his advice. And he addressed it to mother and son together, initially.

"I want you both to remember what I said in the meeting about sin," he told them. "It is because we have a sinful nature that we want to do all kinds of harmful and hurtful things. But remember also that God loved us so much that He sent His Son, Jesus, to die on the cross to put away our sin. And He will save us, and change us, and make us His children if we only believe in Him. The best thing both of you could do would be to trust in Christ. He gave me a new life. And He could do the same for you."

Then turning round to look the boy straight in the eye he said, "And you had better stay off the solvents. No more sniffing. Your next time could be your last time. Do you understand what I mean?"

A sullen nod of the head indicated that the point had penetrated.

Assuming that their conversation was now over, both mother and son rose, and were preparing to go, when Chris addressed the lad again.

"Will you promise me to stay off the stuff, and also warn your pals about it as well?" he persisted.

"I promise," came the whispered answer, then both he and his mother pulled their coats up tightly around them and disappeared out into the night.

Chris, who had half-risen to see them out, sat down again.

There was much to think about.

If that ten-year-old kept his promise it would undoubtedly be a life saved from an early grave.

But it was what he had said about his friends that had stung Chris to the core.

'Most of my friends are at it! And an awful lot of the boys in my class!'

Was this drug problem bigger in Belfast than even he had perceived it to be?

This was a ten-year-old talking!

The encounter with that young boy had made him more convinced than ever that there was 'an open door' for the work he was doing, but had also made him more determined to do even more to contact boys like that if he could.

Before he rose to clear up his bits and pieces he closed his eyes briefly and offered a pithy and passionate prayer.

"Please, Lord, help me to help them even more," was simply what he said.

32

BACK FROM THE BRINK

It was almost midnight one evening in March, 1999.

At almost midnight Chris was just beginning to think of going to bed but it would probably take him another hour and a half to get there.

And at almost midnight the phone rang.

The caller was confused. Chris knew who it was immediately he heard the voice. And he also knew that this caller was in real trouble when he heard the load of nonsense he was talking. He was obviously out of his mind, either very drunk, or high on drugs, or what was even more likely, a combination of both.

Chris tried hard to make some sort of sense of the slurred words and disjointed sentences that the man at the other end of the line was using.

"This is John,"(not his real name) he began. "I was just wanting to say...thank you for...trying to help me..."

Slowly Chris was commencing to piece together what he thought to be the purpose of his call.

Then came another torrent of incomprehensible twaddle.

Chris didn't care. He was determined to stay on that phone for as long as it took. He knew quite well that John was in deep distress.

In the midst of all the gush of gobbledygook there came something else which the patient Chris was able to decipher.

"It was good of you, Chris...and thanks anyway..." John was saying, "but I was just a waste of your time...I am no use to anybody...a no-good 'junkie'..."

During the past three or four years Chris had come across many 'no-good junkies' as John described himself. And he knew what they needed. Time. Patience. Tender loving care. So he talked to John, in an attempt to encourage him. It would be good if he could give him back even the slightest scrap of self-esteem.

Then suddenly John interrupted Chris in his current of counsel.

This time, however, it was not with a flood of folly. There was no stream of stammering stupidity.

The message, though slow to come because of the slowed-down speed of John's mental processes, was clear enough. And chilling in its content.

"So good-bye now Chris," he said, "I am going now...and I don't think... I will ever be... seeing you again. So thanks anyway..."

He then replaced the receiver.

Chris sprang into action.

He knew what the message meant.

It was a cry for help.

John was suicidal.

The man who had entered through 'the open door' to help people like John, didn't have nine-to-five hours. And the door of opportunity, or in this case necessity, in his work, could open at any time of the day. Or night.

Chris had to reach John. As soon as possible. Next morning would definitely be too late. John wouldn't be there, then.

For a number of reasons, Chris was never happy to go and visit men in John's condition, alone, so he phoned Ian Martin, a friend of his from church, and asked if he would accompany him. Ian readily agreed, even though it was nearly midnight, gathering from the note of urgency in Chris's voice that this was a matter needing immediate attention.

It sounded like a matter of life and death.

Which, in fact, it was.

There followed a frantic drive through the silent streets and roads of Northern Ireland until Chris and his companion reached John's house.

When they rang the bell John's father came to the door. He had no idea that John had phoned Chris, but when the situation was explained to him he welcomed the two-men-on-his-doorstep immediately.

Chris knew where John's room was. He had been in it many times before.

John, when they found him, was slumped in a chair, with a bottle of tablets in his hand. He was barely conscious. Chris noticed that his eyes were red and swollen. Obviously he had been crying a lot.

They tried to rouse him, speaking loudly.

"John, this is Chris," his friend-in-need told him. "We are here to help you."

Slowly, John lifted up his head as far as he could, and tried to open his eyes.

"It's no good, Chris," he said, with difficulty.

"How many of those tablets have you taken, John?" Chris asked him.

"Not too many," came the sluggish reply. Then he went on to add, after a long-drawn-out sigh, "Yet."

Knowing that their immediate priority was to obtain that phial of tablets, Chris and his friend began to try to talk John out of his proposed course of action, aware that the dose he had already taken, though not lethal, would probably soon put him over to sleep.

"Why are you doing this, John?" Chris enquired, although he had a very good idea. It was vital to allow John to share his feelings, though. Express himself to someone who knew what it was like, and cared for his condition.

"There is no hope left for me," John replied, struggling to keep focused. "I have nothing left to live for."

Chris knew that this conversation was going to be difficult, for John was so far gone, but he kept at it.

"That's not really true, John," he countered. "You have friends, and family to live for."

A deep silence fell over the room. The kind of silence Chris felt he could almost touch.

Then John opened his eyes again. "I have no friends," he whispered. "My friends...all left me long ago. And my family...my family...I am only an embarrassment to them. You see, Chris..." the gaps between words were becoming even longer. "You see, I ...am the ...cause of ...everybody's misery."

That declaration jarred Chris. For that was how he had felt, exactly, the night he had attempted to take his own life, twelve years before. 'The cause of everybody's misery.'

"I know how you feel, John, I can tell you. I have been there," Chris went on to assure him, gently. "But it's not true. I am your friend. And your family DO care for you."

Silence. Deep silence. Again. John appeared asleep. But he wasn't. Not yet.

He had one more desperate declaration to make.

Although it was now perfectly plain that John was having great difficulty even thinking about anything, not to mention the mental agility required to order his thoughts into expression, he opened his red, heavy eyes, which seemed to be rolling around uncontrollably, and said, his voice barely audible, "Death...would be... better than this."

Ian had been sitting silently, surveying the scene up until that moment. Then he thought it was his turn to contribute.

"No, it wouldn't you know, John," he told him tenderly. "For if you die the way you are, the Bible says you will be in hell. Death would not be better than this."

The truth of those final statements was lost on John. He didn't hear them. He had lapsed into unconsciousness.

When he was sure that John wasn't going to waken up again in the meantime, Chris took the two steps needed across the room to remove the tablet bottle from the lying limp hand.

Although they knew that John's life had been saved, and that he was not in any immediate danger, Chris and his friend decided to stay with him for an hour or two. Just to be there. In case he should wake up. Or in case the family wanted to speak to them.

As he sat there, gazing at the sleeping addict who had been so close to death, Chris felt an uncanny sense of having been through all this before. It was all a mirror image of his own experience.

How John had said he felt was precisely how he had felt. What John had tried to do, was identical in every respect, to what he had tried to do.

And they both had been brought back from the brink.

Chris then remembered all the times after that when God had brought him back from the brink of what had seemed certain death.

Then he reflected on that night in the hospital ward when He had brought him back from the brink of eternal death, through faith in Christ.

He thought, too, of the little red Gideon New Testament which he had been given at school, had carried through teenage, and still had in his pocket.

It was all so wonderful...

A tear welled up in his eye, as he and his friend sat watching the out-of-danger John.

For a split-second, he opened his eyes. Then they closed over again.

He was going to make it.

In the solemn stillness of the middle of the night Chris renewed the vow he had made to God, and to himself, on so many such occasions before.

He would strive to see people like John brought back from the brink of both physical and eternal death, whether day or night, summer or winter, at home or abroad.

For as long as the God who had spared his life, and saved his soul, supplied his strength.

And the Bible, the extra-special book of his boyhood, would be his guiding text.

AMBASSADOR

Belfast Northern Ireland **Greenville** South Carolina

OTHER BOOKS BY THE SAME AUTHOR

MY FATHER'S HAND

THIS IS FOR REAL

JUST THE WAY I AM

SOME PARTY IN HEAVEN

FIRST CITIZEN SMYTH

SOMETHING WORTH LIVING FOR

HOW SWEET THE SOUND

AS OUR HEADS ARE BOWED

ONLY THE BEST WILL DO

A BRUISED REED

OUT OF THE MAZE

THE TANGLED LAMB